VIVENUS:
STARCHILD

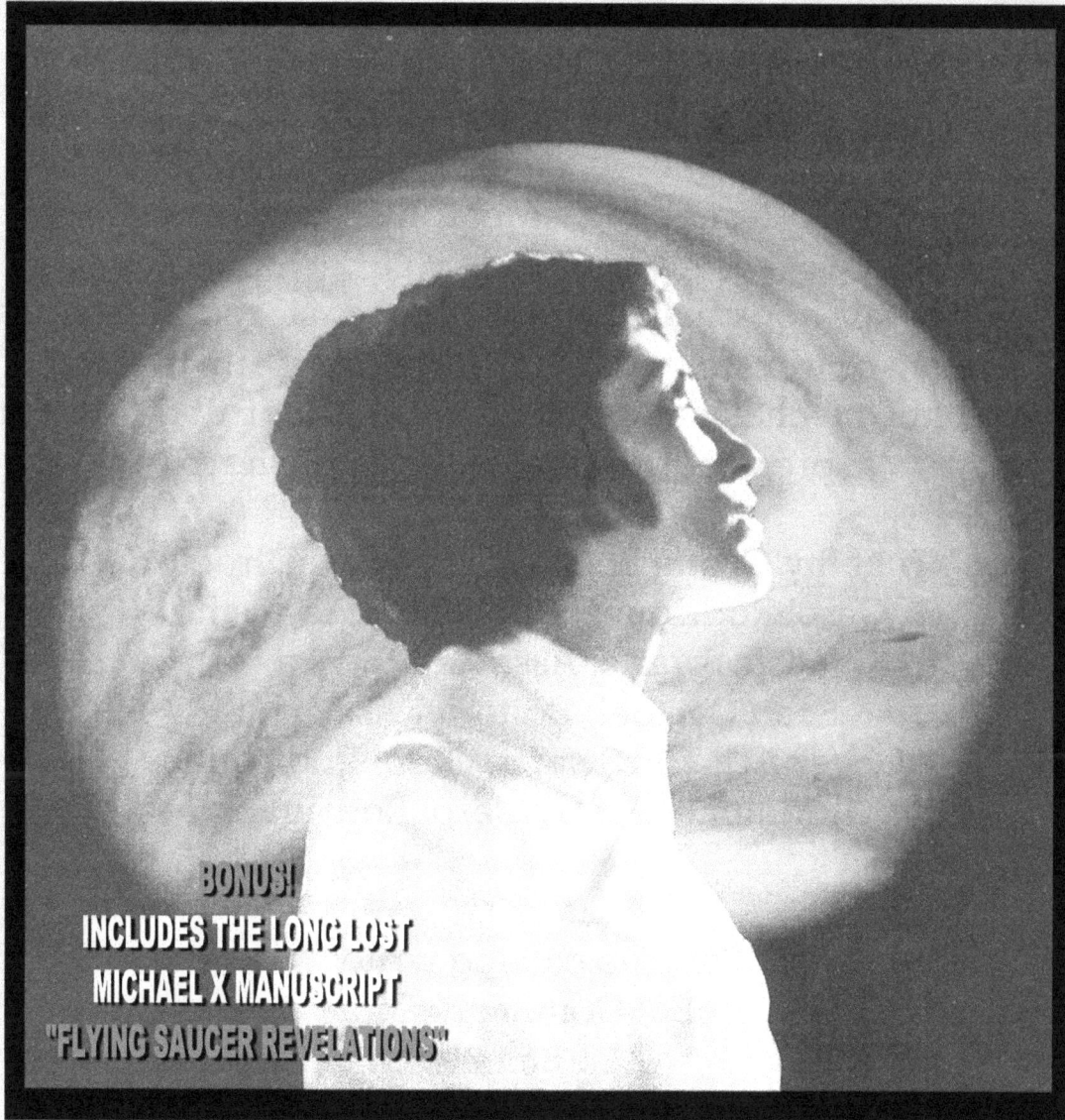

BONUS!
INCLUDES THE LONG LOST
MICHAEL X MANUSCRIPT
"FLYING SAUCER REVELATIONS"

GLOBAL COMMUNICATIONS

Vivenus: Starchild

By Vivenus, Michael Barton, Timothy Green Beckley

ISBN-10: 1-60611-106-X
ISBN-13: 978-1-60611-106-2

Nonfiction – Metaphysics

Timothy Green Beckley: Editorial Director
Carol Rodriguez: Publishers Assistant
Tim Swartz: Associate Editor
Sean Casteel: Editorial Assistant
Cover Art: Tim Swartz, Carol Rodriguez
Additional Art by Carol Rodriguez

For free catalog write:
Global Communications
P.O. Box 753
New Brunswick, NJ 08903

Free Subscription to Conspiracy Journal E-Mail Newsletter
www.conspiracyjournal.com

Vivenus: Starchild

Contents

Vivenus: Starchild

Vivenus – Did She Really Come Here From Venus?

by Timothy Green Beckley

I can't in all honesty tell you I believe her story!

How can a grown, mature, person with all his faculties con

someone into believing they know someone from another planet who is walking our Earth and living amongst us? Science does, after all, tell us life cannot possible exist elsewhere in our own solar system.

Hey, I have a reputation for being pretty straight forward. Some may see me as gullible and overly credulous. Others may think of me as a wide eyed believer of cosmic fairy tales. While a few think I am too "straight laced" in my thinking, and I should drop all credibility and come out full force in favor of just about any lunatic theme you can envision.

Basically, I refuse to be caught up in any of the above.

Each case, each incident --every scenario -- has to be treated on its own merits -- including the account of our very human looking alien friend Vivenus.

I first met this very captivating lady several days before she was to appear at the National UFO Conference, convening at the Hotel Commodore in NY the week of June 24th, 1967 to celebrate the 20th anniversary of Kenneth Arnold's historic UFO sighting over Mt Rainer, Washington. Several evenings before, she had appeared on the Long John Nebel all nite Party Line on WOR Radio as if materializing out of the blue. It was on this program that she told a stunned host and tens of thousands over the airwaves, how she had arrived on Earth leaving her old body behind on Venus, and stepping off a space ship that had landed in Central Park.

Vivenus: Starchild

Vivenus was too good to be true. Who from Venus could speak such perfect English I thought. Must be a scam, a product of Long John's frugal mind meant to draw an ever increasing audience to his weird world midnight till dawn broadcast.

But what Vivenus had to say sounded like it was enchanted. It was pure cosmic poetry. Peace on Earth. Love of our fellow human beings. An end to cruelty and an openness toward other beings said to exist throughout the universe. It was like this lovely lady from off world had the capability to put a spell on others so that they too would turn into believers in her exotic cause.

Over 2000 individuals showed up to hear her speak at Jim Moseley's UFO conference. Not a sound could be heard as she delivered her message to the masses. She stayed upon the New York scene for a few months and than started to travel the country to spread her interplanetary scenario far and wide. For several years the faithful wanted to read what this remarkable woman had to say, but Vivenus seemed to find it difficult to put her story down in words until finally she sent her hand written manuscript to me to retype and put out in book form. The manuscript was relatively small, but each word was heart felt. But Vivenus' word were too late as she had been mostly forgotten by time her personal diary of coming here from "there" appeared in print.

Eventually, Vivenus disappeared apparently for good not answering any of her correspondence sent to a post office box in Florida and collected from time to time. The story went idle. Even those that believed had put her and the fantastic tale of coming from Venus out of their minds.

Now after more than a decade we are bringing her story back so the public can be aware of her intentions while she was on this planet.

Vivenus: Starchild

There are others who have taken over Vivenus' mantel, including Omni Onec whose works we have also published. Her story is strikingly similar to that of Vivenus. But there are many of "them" who claim now to be among us, living here, sharing our culture and our social disquiet. There is the work, for example, of the UMMO group in Spain who have set up an entire city, it is claimed, in several out of the way regions. And we have just recently heard of a group in Italy calling itself "The Friends." Apparently they look almost exactly like us but stand a bit taller or maybe a bit shorter, but not "odd" enough to stand out in a crowd.

The interest of the "aliens amongst us" seems to be positive in nature, as they ostensibly want to guide us to a higher plateau of spirituality and cosmic wisdom. Perhaps their message is still too lofty for us to deal with as we seek out a six pack and watch our favorite Sunday afternoon quarterback for satisfaction.

But who am I to say what is truth and what is fiction. I am only the publisher, your friendly messenger of the weird and bizarre doing his best to speed the asteroids through our atmosphere of confusion. You decide for yourself from reading the words of Vivenus if she is heaven sent or just another whack job from east of the Rockies who claims to have landed in a spaceship now a long time ago in the middle of a deserted New York City park. After all she wouldn't be the first strange person to have come to the Big Apple, now would she?

Tim Beckley, Publisher

MRUFO8@HOTMAIL.COM

www.ConspiracyJournal.Com – free weekly newsletter

Vivenus: Starchild

Are There Aliens Amongst Us?

"It's a part of UFO research you seldom hear about," says Tim Beckley, editor of the Conspiracy Journal. "I have often heard the story of human-looking, "Nordic-like" aliens living among us, having become part of our society without the knowledge of their neighbors. They are even said to have married humans, but remember in Genesis it says that there were giants in the earth in those days and that they mated with the daughters of God who were lovely and fair. The late Dr. Frank Stranges said he had once met a man inside the Pentagon who was from another world who could read minds and had no fingerprints and that there were no wars or crime on their planet. A college professor once told the story about how he had witnessed the landing of a space ship and saw its alien crew members emerge and drive off in an American-made automobile, only to see one of them standing in a supermarket line shortly thereafter.

"But the cases like those of Omnec Onec, a beautiful 'ambassador from Venus,' are infrequent, but they do exist," confirms Beckley.

They came physically from Venus in the great vimanas of Vedic and Atlantean literature, and some of them also took physical incarnation on this planet. They claim to have designed and constructed or guided the construction of several of the great pyramids of the world, some of which still remain undiscovered. They introduced or were responsible for the introduction of many of the religions of the world. They designed the 22 highly symbolic pictures painted on the walls of the chamber of initiation in the great pyramid at Ghiza, which later became the court cards of the Egyptian Tarot and the foundation for all other tarot systems known today.

This unique book is the personal account of a living human being who was, with her full consent and active cooperation, transported to Earth in a spacecraft from her home planet. She arrived in the company of her paternal uncle and was carefully prepared and conditioned to live here and grow in the physical society of our native lifewave of our planet.

Her own mother on Venus died shortly after her birth and she was taken into the childless family of her natural mother's sister and raised as her own. When her uncle accepted a mission to the denser lifewave of Earth she chose to come along in order to make up some lapses in her own experience in the denser physical realm and to balance some unfinished Karma, both physically and with other personalities here.

She was carefully conditioned to our density and became physically manifest in an Earth-body equivalent to a 7 year old girl. Her uncle and the crew brought her here, introduced her into a Tennessee family who had just lost their own 7 year old daughter, Sheila, in a terrible bus accident enroute to her grand-mother's home to go to school. The grandmother, having seen little of the granddaughter, was not aware of the substitution, and sent the Venusian to school as her own kin. Years later Sheila's adopted mother was made aware of the substitution by the Venusian uncle, who explained everything to her, and she agreed to raise Omnec Onec in place of her own daughter Sheila.

Although Omnec had the appearance of a 7 year old girl she had the Venusian wisdom and knowledge of her 210 Earth-year equivalent at the time of her arrival here in 1955. This enabled her brilliance in school and she excelled in almost everything, which she tried to conceal so as to protect her real identity.

This, then, is the story of her early life on Venus, her arrival here in the middle of our first modern excitement over UFOs, her preparation and adaptation to Earth living and its peculiar problems, unknown to her on her home planet.

But how is this possible? How can we reconcile this report with the severely inhospitable conditions perceived and measured by science as surface conditions of Venus?

Omnec Onec {Sheila} makes reference in this book to land and water separation, and to bases and structures on her home planet, Venus, as well as on Mars and our own Moon. We see no evidence of structures or of artificial organization on either Venus or our moon or Mars, two of which have been completely photographed with high resolution cameras.

We also fail to see the seas and rivers, and bridges and port facilities that certainly should have shown up within the camera resolution available.

This seems to be an irreconcilable problem on the face of it and casts the rest of the story into serious doubt for much of our unenlightened Earth humanity. But is this a necessary situation? There are very broad-based beliefs in earth society that have been with us through all our history, that easily accomodate the seeming conflict between this account and our contemporary view of our reality.

Some Eastern beliefs allow for an unseen astral world that co-exists in time and space with us, which has form and structure and is peopled with beings, both good and bad, who are aware of us and can and do influence us.

The theosophists studied those concepts with a scientific fervor and attempted to explain them in technical terms and to relate this underlying nature to the physical sciences we thought we knew.

The First Principles of Theosophy by Jinradasa, originally published in Adhyar, India, provided one of the most authoritative early treatises on the nature of beinq for Earth humanity.

The Freemasons originating in Europe propounded similar ideas in great secrecy. The Rosicrucians shared a common origin with Freemasonry but published their ideas more openly.

In a volume called, *"The Cosmoconception"* by Max Heindel, many of the great mysteries of being were described in contemporary Western language, and again was related to science. There are many such references in metaphysical literature. Eduard Schare in France and Rudolf Steiner in Germany wrote extensively on such meta-physical concepts and understanding.

All of these great schcols of thought divided the nature of being into several planes of existence, the lowest and densest for us being the physical plane. They divide the physical plane into 7 levels of density: solids, liquids, gasses, plasma state (a sort of supergas) or 4th etheric, 3rd etheric, 2nd etheric and 1st etheric.

All of these states, we are told, are still of the physical plane making up the form world, and they all have density, form, rigidity, mass, weight, inertia and other properties of physical plane matter appropriate to the nature of their state. There is for most of us an apparent major division along these seven states of matter. The lower three are called, for the sake of convenience, the form world, or the 3-

dirnensional world, or the third density, the only world to us as denizens of that realm.

Though we really occupy all of those states of the plane simultaneously, w are only aware on the lower 3 planes. Another with a greater awareness may not be familiar with our limitations because they "see" more of the total reality. We cannot see the additional reality that they see because of our own limitations in perception and we reject that part of existence. This does not make it any less real, however, and as our awareness improves we will be able to "see" more.

We have designed very sophisticated instruments to extend our perceptions and have made high resolution images of the moon and Mars from which we may study the lower 3 states of matter. A complex of buildings or a planned structured facility on these levels would surely show up. And, much as we would like to believe it, all scientists are not in on a cover-up. We have a complete file of Moon photos, tens of thousands of them, all automatically numbered by the cameras as the pictures were taken. The same goes for Mars. They are all here, including the mis-shot frames, and still no cities on the moon, no oceans and ports on Mars. Others can study these files and come up with the same conclusions. In 5 or 10 years the low level orbiters will photograph every inch of Venus, and whatever they find will so similarly be made available to researchers. They are not expected to "see" much more than already revealed on the moon and Mars.

Until our awareness increases, however, and we develop the instruments and evolve the senses to extend our awareness, we still will have only the lower form states to study, which may not be where the action is at the present time. If, however, the primary existence, structures and appurtenances of that place are on a different level of the forms (physical) that are found on Earth, then we may be completely unaware of them although they may exist right here as one or more parallel universes.

VIVENUS: STARCHILD

Vivenus: Starchild

CONTENTS

COVER & INSIDE ART BY: CAROL ANN RODRIGUEZ

DESIGN AND LAYOUT: BARBARA LEEDS

SPECIAL ASSISTANCE: BARBARA GRAHAM

Published by:

GLOBAL COMMUNICATIONS

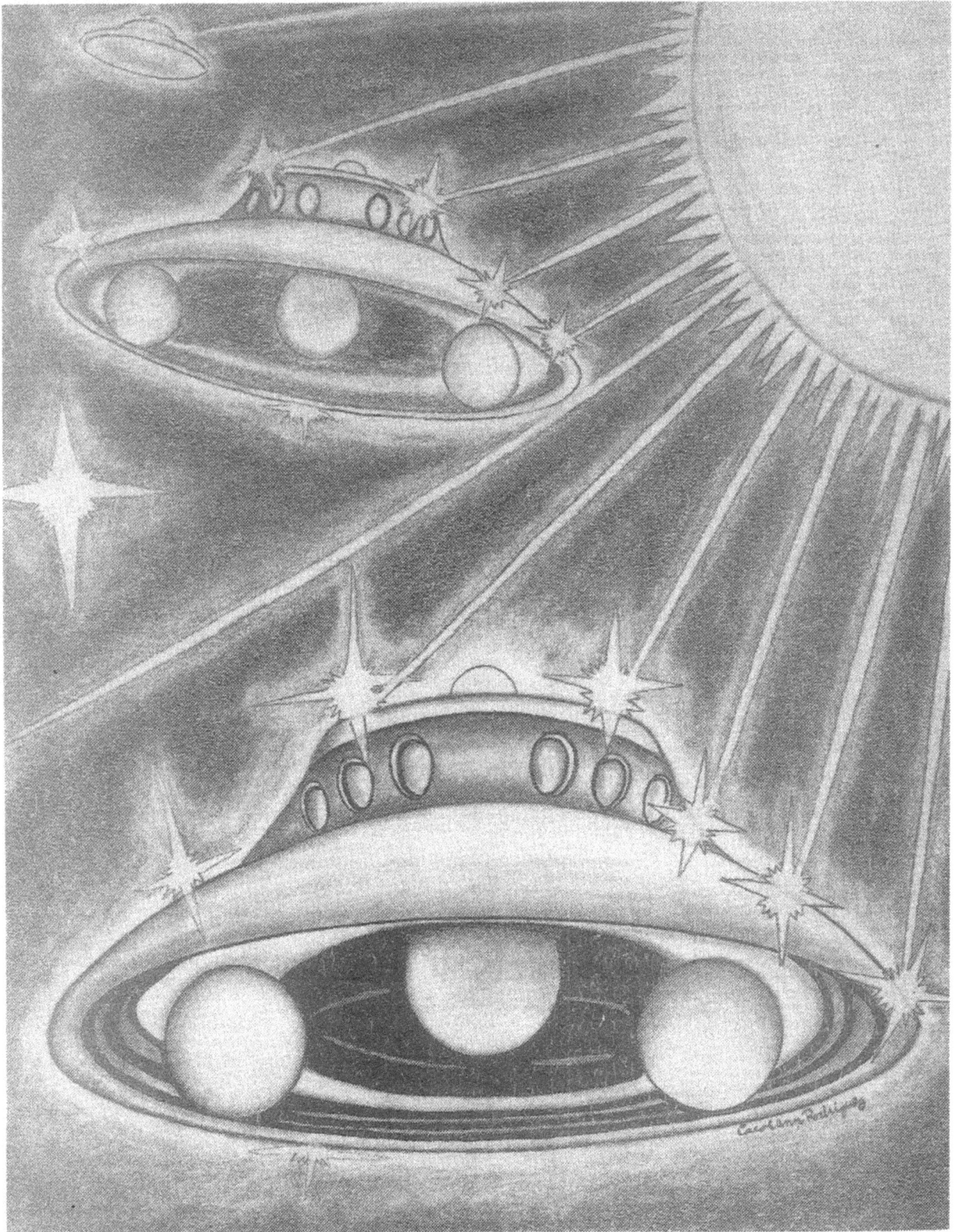

Vivenus: Starchild

VENUS HOME STAR

CITIES OF LIGHT
DAYS WITHOUT NIGHT
CITIES OF GOLD
TIME WITHOUT OLD
REASONS OF PURE
ENTITY SURE
LOVE AND TO FEEL
LIGHT AND WHAT'S REAL
WORDLESS AND SILENT
AND FREE JUST TO BE
TRUE TO LIFE'S SPIRIT
NOT A "ME" - BUT A "WE"
CITIES OF LIGHT
LIVING BY RIGHT
LOVE RULES OUR LAND
AND WE OFFER OUR HAND.

Vivenus: Starchild

A SPECIAL PRAYER

Dear Father, in heaven, in earth, in me. How important is "a book" in Thy plan? You know, dear Lord, it was never any secret desire of mine to write one.

Do You want Thy children upon the Earth plane to become conscious of details about life on another world You created? Will it help them to see the light and come to the light more quickly?

We know, O' Lord, what the doubters will do to a book such as this.We know, O' Lord that there will be sounds of laughter every-where throughout the Earth. And yet, for those on Earth who want to rise to light - want to believe in Thy plan of love, it is for them Ye save the cities, and it is for them, I have come.

How long must the light be slighted to prevent the ridicule of the darkness? Is now the time the light is acknowledged and encouraged and concentrated upon?

It is hard, Lord, to put into words my life that began on a word-less world. How shall I give names to things and "people" that had none? How is beauty defined and labeled? How is peace described in detail? And how shall Venusian memories be translated into the Earth language?

If this book of Venus and "me" truly is Thy will, then help Thou me O' Love, that through it, I may glorify Thee and speed Thy plan for Earth.

I pray. In the name of the Prince of Love - "Jesus", I so ask.

(4)

Vivenus: Starchild

INTRODUCTION

VENUS MY HOME

Dear friend in light, as you read this let the light glow brighter within you.

Please understand that what I shall share here, I must translate into the Earth tongue. I must - against the natural grain of me, name and label and classify in words the life I lived at home. I must seem to bottle and confine beauty as though it could be. It is a strange task and I pray I can achieve it.

We are free at home - not stopped by the policemen of words. We do not name beauty, but become one with it. And we do not question joy, but just enjoy it.

We have not "time". We live in the eternal now, so it will be difficult to pinpoint events and memories and celebrations. But divine love will give to me what I need, if you will keep in your mind all along these pages, that Venus is a wordless world, a silent world. When we communicate at home, it is not by sound but by feeling. And if memory restores some "conversations" in this writing, understand it was not actually in words, but in feeling that I must put into words.

I shall describe scenery, places, souls and moments in my Venusian life, and it shall surprise me if I can do it because at home I never had to put into words what was in my heart. What we do at home is flow in feelings which turns into a state of being called love.

The "things" on Venus are not really "things" as they seem to be on Earth. We make what we make for the most part, with our minds. No sounds of hammers pounding nails. We vision our house, and the house is there. We can envision its being built "brick by brick" or we can see it all at once perfect and complete.

ARRIVAL ON EARTH

My name is Viv. Full name is VIVenus. This is my soul name, the one I was given for my mission of Earth. And I was given this name on the planet Venus where I was born.

I cannot prove my origin. I cannot prove that what I share with you is true about my heavenly home. I cannot even prove that I exist at all. Perhaps I am but a figment of your imagination. What is proof, is an illusion of the mind. What is faith is of the heart and thus, is real. If I do exist, then I am from Venus. I have no credentials, but one: my heart that does not stop loving you, oh, child on Earth.

Before I came to the Earth plane, when I was at home on Venus, I had a vision of all of you. I felt that the Earth would welcome - if not me - then the truths I would discover, to help them find the peace

and inner contentment, independent of what happens on the outside.
But now I know my vision was a mirage. The Earth seems satisfied to
resign itself to depression, despair...dead ends. Does this planet
Earth need me from Venus? Did it ever need me? I still don't know...

```
          THE CHRISTMAS TREE ADORNED
          WITH ORNAMENTS AND TINSEL
          BLINKING COLOR LIGHTS, CANDY CANES
          IS SOMEHOW NOT COMPLETE
          UNTIL THE STAR IS PLACED ON TOP.

          PERHAPS I AM THE TINSEL.
          PERHAPS A CANDY CANE.
          PERHAPS ONE LIGHT
          PERHAPS ONE NEEDLE OF THE TREE.
          BUT I AM NECESSARY
          FOR I AM THERE.
```

MISSION OF LOVE

The planet Earth waits for a God of love to wave His magic wand
and bless the land making all sorrow, sickness, evil go away. The
planet Earth waits and waits, and we, not from planet Earth, are here
to warn you - not to wait. The God event you anticipate for the Earth,
must happen first - within you.

Yes, there are others here on Earth from other worlds. I am not
the only one on love's mission. Love has its helpmates in every field -
in every country in your world. Not all entered the earth atmosphere
as I entered, and we each have our roles to play.

I have stayed away from my home for I did not want to do,
consciously, anything you, O' Earth, do not consciously think you can
do. My mission is not necessarily to do "one great thing" that those
of Earth may gasp - but my mission is to awake the children of Earth
to the reality of love. Yes, how you, O' Earth can live by love and
obey its laws and change the Earth to a planet.. "on Earth..as it is
in heaven..."

We upon the Earth, not from the Earth, and you from the Earth who
are awake...seem to be held back from stopping the legions of darkness
to seem to prosper. We each are given our tasks for the day..and
through these tasks, let our God do the real work.

We, from the light worlds, have been trained in silence, and
prayer, and not being very aggressive - nor combative - we have learned
to "turn the other cheek"...to "forgive seventy times seven"..to "agree
with our adversary while we are in the way with him"...

I made waves once on Earth, and then let the sea calm. Now shall
I seem to make waves again? So be it, if it is the will of love.

(6)

Vivenus: Starchild

The planet Earth has light upon it, and love, and even though
the darkness and evil is louder and thus, given more attention, does
it truly outnumber the light?

We from other worlds do not believe so, and I feel in my soul
that if and when the children of light on Earth realize how they, you,
would and will rise to the occasion.

You know the truth to set you free. It is not new. You recognize
justice and right and believe in perfection without anyone outside
of your being teaching you. The truth is born within you, as God,
and love is born within you. It's something you automatically know
deep inside.

But, O' Earth, you do not know how to apply that right, that
justice of love, that perfection to your life here in the Earthly
dramas.

Who speaks to you today, for many centuries, speaks from a cloud
way above you. Have they stood on the step you're standing on now?
Can they tell you how to reach your star from where you are now.

WHEN THE EARTH BECOMES QUICKSAND,
REACH NOT FOR A BRANCH, IT WILL BREAK.
LOOK NOT TO THE PERSON NEXT TO YOU
HE IS SINKING, TOO.
LOOK NOT TO THE PERSON WALKING ON A CLOUD
SHE WILL NOT GET HER HANDS DIRTY.
NO, WHEN THE EARTH BECOMES QUICKSAND
LOOK TO THE PERSON WHO WAS SENT TO THIS EARTH
TO BE SO SWALLOWED
THAT SHE COULD LEARN TO RISE ABOVE
THAT SHE COULD THEN, GUIDE YOU.

THE PLAN

It feels like it would be easy to come from a perfect world and
instantly "give a message" of hope and faith to Earth, a message which
the hearts of Earth already know, though the minds of Earth will not
believe. Doctors and nurses on The Earth to help the people whose
flesh is sick, read books about the sickness. They study other people's
sickness. They practice on other people's sickness.

Doctors and nurses sent down from heaven to heal the souls agree
to take on the very sickness into their own souls, and by the laws
of love, learn how to heal themselves, that they, in turn can help
those sick, be their own physicians.

The Earth people are trained too well to count on help from
someone, something outside them. And we, from Venus, and other worlds

(7)

Vivenus: Starchild

must stay in the background as long as possible, that we add not to the Earth condition.

The role of "leader" defies the very instruction of the role. Yet, someone has to tell you what you already know.

Someone has to love you. Someone has to sing to you the song of reality. Someone has to play the part assigned to her. It is the plan.

Years ago (in 1967) as I stood on a stage at a giant flying saucer convention in New York City, it bothered me that the children of Earth were more interested in Venus and me, than in the message I brought to them. But now (1982) it does not bother me: for after so many years of survival and mission in this cold world, I understand with my heart one more dimension of your heart, that I did not understand then, the need to believe in or become fascinated by a better world. For it is so easy to just give up on this one. But you know, we mustn't.

```
IN THE SECRET WORLD OF TINY GLITTERING STARS,
ONE WORLD WOULD ITS VOICE.
IT WHISPERS: "I AM VENUS..LAND OF LOVE.
LAND OF PINK SKIES AND SOFT WHITE GRASS.
I AM VENUS, LAND OF LIGHT
WHERE THERE IS NEVER NIGHT.
VENUS..I AM VENUS, WHAT AM I THEN TO YOU?
I AM A WORLD WHEREIN YOU MAY LIVE TRULY
IN YOUR PRETENDING ALL IS RIGHT, ALL IS GOOD,
ALL IS WELL.
I AM VENUS, LAND OF LOVE.
NOT AS THE EARTH KNOWS LOVE
BUT AS THE EARTH KNOWS..GOD IS LOVE.

PLANET OF EARTH WHERE GOOD IS RESISTED
AND GIFTS FROM LOVE DENIED AND QUESTIONED.
SHALL WE LEAVE YOU ALONE TO WORK OUT YOUR "DISASTERS"?
SHALL WE LEAVE YOU IN PAIN AS YOU WORK THROUGH THEM
TO THE CONCLUSION THAT LOVE IS ALL THAT CAN
ENDURE AND LAST..?

THE SECRETS OF THE UNIVERSE ARE NOT IN THESE PAGES
BUT IN THE SILENT PAGES OF YOUR HEART.

VENUS..I AM VENUS, LAND OF LOVE.
```

(8)

Vivenus: Starchild

CHAPTER ONE

BEING BORN ON VENUS

Born on the planet Venus. There was no year, for only the Earth counts measures and miles. Perhaps a day on Earth is but a moment in the eternal spheres. Perhaps the night only comes to a planet that needs to close its eyes that it may awake.

Eternity, one long forever. No sense, no need to slice it up into little pieces; to say this is a "year", this is a "month", this is a "day". Eternity, the real time on Venus, and so the "year" I was "born" as VIVenus upon it, I do not honestly know, was not told, do not need to know. I do know that when America was born, I was already in existence on my Venus, Home Star, because I heard its initial vows. Great moments of light reach our world and touch our hearts and we kneel in prayer and we bless the blessing sent to us.

I do remember being born on Venus and being re-born on Venus several times. Angels singing and the touch of the Father's hand to awake me into a beautiful land of pinks and golds and pure, pure whites. And then the whites would disunite and every color love ever made, danced before my eyes. I remember the feeling of warm comforting love and any flashbacks of where I had been, were just not there.

Several journeys have I made to planet Earth, each on a mission of divine love. Each time, wearing a different disguise, each time, playing a different role and each time I was returned home to be born again but not as an infant, but as the full grown soul I was.

To share with you my very first beginnings on the planet Venus when I was a child and lived as a child until I was a child no more, please bear with me. For just as your memories of your beginnings, some moments are vivid within the soul, some moments you "never forget" but some moments are too sacred and too private to share. But I will do my best and share as much as is comfortable within my soul.

I shall begin with my "family", though all children of God are my relations and all who love love are my kin. I did have an "immediate" family. Two parents, who guided me, encouraged me, trusted me, gave to me, showed me, loved me; and two brothers, Rani and Donnelle, who cradled me, played with me, laughed with me, taught me, loved me. My Venus family. We have not been "in touch" during my waking hours upon this Earth in this role I play this lifetime; but only during my "sleep" hours, and most times, I did not return of a morning with recall. Yet, some days ago, because this book is upon me, I consciously contacted my Venusian family and brought them to me. And they, with their Love for me and for you, channelled a writing that they offered to include here.

"Dear sister, a long way from us, but so close

(9)

Vivenus: Starchild

in our hearts and right before our eyes right
now. You wanted to feel what they feel on Earth
...and so you have. But do not let it get the
best of you. Do not go as far as they go.
Sink no more into the quicksand.
Depression is a heavy cloud over the Earth,
and we in our swoops can not see clearly
through the cloud. We must penetrate
this cloud, and we come to you, our sister,
to ask your help. Donnelle and I are right
above you, watching over you, and watching
over the Earth.

When we left you there, we at once realized
our mission too. We all work together
preparing for the time love shall light
the Earth. So if thy torch has become heavy,
feel our hands around thine, helping thee
to lift it ..."

                        with all our love,

                        Rani and Donnelle

"Dear daughter, you did not go to the Earth
to "fit in", but to take charge of all in
your fields. To lift, to inspire, to
rekindle hope. We, staying home and
journeying nowhere, had lost vision of you
for awhile. And we know now it was because
you, messenger of light, had slipped into
depression and despair. But enough, dear
daughter. We cannot welcome you back in
that state. You know the rules, and the laws
on our home planet. Realize again who you are.
Realize again from where you have been sent
and why, and be patient yet a little more.
Your destiny is a fact of life and we have
no third team to rescue you, who was the second
team. So please, dear daughter, think of us now
more often. Allow yourself the luxury of
calling on those who love you and stand by
to assist you. It is not an unfair advantage,
you have earned the gold.

Let all worlds become one and we pray you get
every help you need to lighten the planet with
love. You were born for this mission. It is
time you took a firmer hold onto the torch.
And know ye, dear daughter, our hands shall
entwine thine, to help thee lift it high
all for the glory of our Almighty God

(10)

- 10 -

Vivenus: Starchild

and the Prince of Love, the one who was
Jesus The Chirst upon the Earth."

with all our love

your Mother, and Papa.

GROWING AS A CHILD

Childhood on Venus, a time of nurturing and cradling love.
A time to be shown all the beauty the Father has given, not my
"immediate" papa, but the Father whom you know as "God". Childhood
on Venus; a time to see the land He has placed us upon. A time of
feeling close to the Creator. A time of wonder, of suspense and
surprises. A time of joy and laughter and singing.

As I single out my family on Venus, recognize that ours was
not the exception to the rule, that all life on Venus is surrounded
by love and all families live in the state of perfection. Perfect
love as the Father created it.

We are individuals and each a unique expression of the love
that made us and we each, when we are brought together, bring out
another aspect of the love we individually are. My family made me
feel so at peace, so one with the oneness and they brought forth from
me, from that peace I felt, a gentle expression.

As an infant, I did not have to learn any words. I did not ever
cry. I was not ever hungry. I was held and rocked and fed with love.

Once my papa carried me to the edges of Venus and showed me our
universe. And then he set me down. And though my feet did not touch
our ground, I did not fall. I walked as Venusians walk, I ran as
Venusians run, just a little bit above the ground.

The first time I touched a tree, a silver tree with leaves all
colors, it reached out its arms to me. It lowered one of its "branches"
and scooped me up onto it and there I saw for the first time my
whole world of Venus, Home Star.

At home, we revere the tree. The trees are our cathedrals. We
do not climb them nor frolic around them. They glow a light and we enter
into that light for the blessing of purity.

The spirit of Venus is freedom. We live without fear. We expect
not ever any harm to come to us. And it doesn't. My parents did not
police me and did not ever make me feel less important than they. They
always told me that what I felt was right and they encouraged me to
act it out. Sometimes they "told" me "no" but with it, exchanged a "yes".
The "no" came because I would not finish a feeling through but too
soon, too soon, leap on to the next one. I was full of questions,

(11)

- 11 -

ideas, curiosities and my loving parents felt to slow me down. They kept reminding me I had eternity, I had forever and one time my mother said that I would miss the best part of the changing sky if I looked away too soon.

My brothers were always making me feel extra joyful. I did not try to be grown up with them, but instead they became as young as I. We played somersaults and circles 'round' - a game where we would spin around and around and around and begin to lift further off our Venusian ground, and then when we were high enough, we'd circle down.

There is never any nighttime on Venus, tho' every so often the pastel pink sky glows pale. In these ultra-quiet times, my parents, my brothers and I would gather into a circle, hold each others hands and thank our Father for life. And then we would set ourselves down on our Venus land, ground ourselves and rest for awhile.

These times were the hardest for me, for I did not want to rest. I wanted to keep moving and enjoying and exploring.

But my parents and my brothers taught me to be still. They promised in the stillness I would dicover something. I did. It was a brand new silence. It was pretty and so soft. I guess I could call it the sweet glow of thank you.

We each lifted from our rest at the same moment, and the sky was bright again. We prayed another thank you to begin our "day". Sometimes we'd "plan" a "picnic" in our deep blue-silver forest or a sailboat parade upon our pink lake. Many times we left each other "alone" to do whatever only "alone" can do.

LIFE WITHIN THE FAMILY

We lived in a house, a house made of a clay-like substance in the shape of bricks, yellow bricks. Soft to the touch, fragrant like a sweet, red rose. My house at home is pale yellow, four windows without glass in them, two doors without locks, no curtains, no roof, no floor.

We were not "poor" but simply in keeping with the "style" on Venus. Why shut out the glorious sky with all its changing colors? It will never rain, never snow, never be too cold, never be too windy. And no world of sun on Venus to scorch us. The soft, white grass of home cannot ever be covered. It is sacred ground. We do not wear shoes, for the touch of our sacred ground is blessed when we are moved to touch it. My house has a room for each of us (five in all) plus a big room where we all gather together.

We have no radio, no TV, no telephone. We entertain each other. And most of all, we just love being together.

My brothers left home (our house) for awhile. Where they went, I knew not. They didn't announce their going; they just went. I was

(12)

surprised not to see them. I could have tuned in to them and called their attention to me, but I felt not to. My mother tuned in to me and assured me they would return.

While my brothers were away, my parents took me places all over our world. The three of us walked ("floated") hand in hand. Sometimes they would swing me between them. Sometimes they would turn me in a direction and show me something even more wondrous than what was right in front of me. One time, a little blue pony appeared and seemed to follow us for awhile. Then he led us to a field of lilac flowers and beyond the flowers, were more ponies, some blue, some light green, some pink, some cheerful yellow. And then our little blue pony friend lifted his head, said something in his own special way and trotted beyond the lilac flowers to his pony friends.

During that special time of "sight-seeing", my parents took me to visit all their friends which, on Venus, means: every soul who lives upon the planet. I was introduced to the whole world of Venus and my parents told me that these friends of theirs were my friends, too. In fact, in truth, they were more than friends but were and are another part of my family.

The homes we visited felt familiar, yet there were not two colors or two designs alike. Some were striped like rainbows. Some were little circles inside of bigger circles. Our house was (is) shaped like an almond and other houses shaped, one like a canoe; one like a horse, so different, yet every house fragrantly scented and cozy with love.

No ones immediate family seemed to have more than three children and most had only one.

Our journey of exploration and visiting had its duration. It was time to return to our own house. But to get back, we were not to "walk". My parents told me to close my eyes and picture our little house - every room - every detail - to picture it strongly and to see myself with them sitting in our big gathering together room. I did as they told me, closed my eyes, shut out where I was and pictured where I wanted to be, with them there too. And they must have made the picture, too; for in an instant, we were exactly where I had pictured us to be, in our big gathering together room in our house.

We have what is like sort of a "piano" in there. Each of us could play it when we were moved to. It has many more keys than the piano on Earth, and the keys on our piano are ivory and gold. My papa loved to play our piano more than any of us. Sometimes we would sit and listen, and sometimes we would each stay in our own world of being and actually not hear him.

My mother liked to paint, usually it was a portrait of someone we had never seen. She did not paint on paper but on a special fabric she invented, one that would in a moment with a touch of her hand -

(13)

erase something she did not want there. The paint was something she did not want there. The paint was smooth and dried at once. The fragrance of the paint that lingered even after the painting was done seemed somehow an invitation to look.

My parents sometimes left our house without me and when they did, one of our friends would appear to look in on me. If my parents were gone more than long and right up into the dimming of our pastel sky, a whole family of friends would appear and have me join their "thank you, Father, for life, good evening" prayer. Then we would rest together and when "the new day" glowed bright, my parents were there beside me to greet it.

I know not in numbers just how "long" I was a child at my house but it was as long as I needed it to be. Each child on Venus is a child until his or her moment of realization comes, that he or she has a responsibility to life. It is a moment of wanting to give, that comes when a flash of pictures floods your mind of all the gifts given to you. Not all of us "grow up" at the same time in eternity and some have chosen to be children forever. It is a wonderful life, a life that brings joy to all.

We do have "school" on Venus, but not as the Earth knows school. I did not go to one building for so many moments before the sky dimmed. I did not get graded. I did not have to compete. I did not have to learn what did not interest me. There is no math for those not intrigued by numbers. There is no science for those not fascinated by the how it is done. I did not study other people's ideas. I was encouraged to find my own and develop them. I did learn (because I wanted to) the history of my world which began in love and light and then for a time darkness was allowed its visit and then how we returned to love and light where darkness is no more.

There was music and games and lighting and lifting and baking and building, everything for everybody and everything for every interest.

THE EDUCATION OF ONE'S SELF

The beginning school on Venus is a village unto itself. We live away from our immediate family during this schooling and we do not see them again until the "graduation".

My "first day" at school and away from home without my parents to tune in to, was a day that made me feel even closer to them, somehow. And the "longer" we were "apart" the stronger was my feeling of love for them. I did not "miss" them for I felt them in my heart as a part of me and though I was not allowed to tune in to them and thus, break from where I was and my soul wanted to be, nevertheless, I could feel their love for me growing stronger too. It was and is even more so now a love that needed no pictures.

The beginning school on Venus is a small replica of the land of

(14)

Vivenus: Starchild

Venus, the world of Venus. It has many small buildings (without roofs, without floors), representing each village on Venus. Each village on Venus is a specialty unto itself of living, doing, being. And so it is with each small building in our beginning school.

And just as we have a kind of a "mayor" in each village on Venus, so we had a kind of a "teacher" in each building at school. One who called the village occupants to a unified prayer. We did not have desks and when we sat, we sat on our floorless floors. Sometimes an adult soul would communicate to us all at once. But for the most part, it was an individual matter.

For every child on Venus, there is his or her own private counselor, someone assigned to and specialized and trained in the child he or she was born to serve. And not until that child "graduated", did the counselor take on a new assignment.

A counselor is also a friend and did not force us to learn anything. My counselor knew me very well and would present pictures to me right before I would ask for them. He told me what I was, what I had been and what I would become. He told me the story of all worlds, all life, all love but one. But he did not say which one, he only asked me to pray.

Once when I was a child at my house, before I went to beginning school, I felt a pull from a faraway place and I heard a voice crying "help us", help us", I did not know what the word meant, but I felt a sudden longing to be somewhere else. It only happened once when I was at my house before I went to school. And it was too brief a moment for me to explore. It came again at beginning school, the pull from a faraway place and the voice "help us, help us", and the feeling, the longing to be somewhere else. The voice faded out but the feeling lingered and I had to explore it.

My counselor appeared and led me to a building in our school village that represented the planet Earth, and said that this was the world we had prayed for. I shared with him of the voice I had heard two times now from a faraway place. He nodded and smiled, "just as I heard yours". I did not enter that building right then, for I still wanted to be a child.

I remembered my parents telling me on our walks around our world that there was a special reason I was born unto them and especially unto life. They said I had a destiny and a special purpose in our Father's plan and that the most important curiosity I had would be to find out about it. I remembered asking them what it was and they would not tell me. I tried asking my counselor if he knew and he would not tell me, either.

The buildings on Venus are all "sound-proof". I suppose our outdoors is, too, for when we communicate one to one, no one else can hear us. Sounds of laughter, if you want to hear that, can be heard any-

(15)

Vivenus: Starchild

where in Beginning School Village. And if you want to hear the angels, you can hear that too. But Beginning School Village is only a slight bit less silent than our world of Venus.

We had a school yard, many in fact. We had a play field where we could play the games we invented. We had swings to swing on and fly from. We had slides that slid across half our planet and another slide to return us. Stairways that seem to be as high as our sky could reach; little bicycles with but one wheel. One game I always liked was to disappear and reappear as myself or as someone else.

Beginning school was the first time I had learned to make a thing with my mind. It was a carousel - ponies and unicorns on a circle stage, all of it made of crystal. It went around and around and I put music to it. I watched it for a while and then I jumped on and then I called to someone in the schoolyard, and they saw it and glowed and they jumped onto my carousel with me.

All my "days" at beginning school, I followed the spirit of life wherever it led me. Some of my pursuings were long, some short. Every so often, I would return to the building that represented the planet Earth and stand outside its door.

One time that I did this a song bird appeared to me. He was no bigger than my littlest finger. His color was deep, deep blue except for wings that were white. He circled around and around me and around me three times and then invited me to follow him. I floated swiftly as though skating without ice right behind the little song bird. He stopped at a silver tree, perched upon its branch and invited me up.

I closed my eyes and pictured myself upon that silver branch of the silver tree, right beside the song bird. And suddenly, there I was. I laughed and the little song bird sang. And then I began singing with him songs of joy without any words. And I was so happy (feeling so happy) that when our songfest was over, I built for the little songbird with my mind, a little house for him to thank him.

The animals on Venus are so very special as most are on Earth. On Venus they are all pets, though no one "owns" any. They are free, just as we are, to go wherever their love calls them. Most of the pets at home have assignments on the planet Earth. They do not stay long, for they are not as equipped as the souls to endure the vibrations of Earth. But in their short stays, they accomplish much in bringing forth love. At home, there are many varieties of animals and a dog on Earth, may be a cat in heaven. And a cat on Earth may be more than a cat at home. Our cats fly, our puppies don't bark, our tigers don't roar, our birds don't steal from one another. We have seagulls, though we have no sea and swans and ducks that quack only when asked to. All sizes, all brands, all shapes, all colors, all expressions of a peaceful love. Snow white deer, pastel ponies, peach-colored bunny rabbits and all are friends with one another, even the golden lion that plays with the soft, white lamb. Each pet glows of its own

(16)

Vivenus: Starchild

light and through each light glows a rainbow blending with its individual color, that radiates upon our land.

There was one special cat that liked to come to our house. He was gold and white with deep green eyes. He was a special friend to me and as a child, we played a lot together. We also were quiet a lot together. He didn't ever sleep, but he did disappear a lot. On the day I left for school village, he stood upon my foot and would not budge. And then I realized he wanted to come with me. And so he walked with me all the way up to the entrance of school village. I called him Panion. Panion did not enter the school grounds with me but I felt he would be at our house when I returned there.

We don't have mirrors on Venus. So we don't know what we look like unless we go to a lake to see our reflection. And at school village, was the first time I saw a "me" that I knew was a "me". I remember the surprise of it.

At beginning school on Venus, no one is left out and all are "popular". Privacy of spirit is what we learn at our school. Learning not to intrude on another's space of being when he or she needs aloneness in the light. We are taught to recognize the faint barrier of a light stream and to recognize it as a sign not to trespass there.

Two children in this cycle of growing were closest to me, and I to them. One, named Anna and the other named, Timot. When we were with each other, we would automatically know when to "stay away". We were a natural team in understanding each other's beings. Anna had a strength of spirit, an expression of a jubilee, enthusiastic and glowing in joy. And Timot daring and free who liked to fly from tree to tree. We shared our curiosities about our "futures", our destinies, and we felt somehow our destinies were linked, but perhaps this was the beginning to that awareness.

We created things with our minds; shoes and kites and tiny buildings; "roller coasters" and "ice cream cones" and hats and wings and all kinds of wondrous and silly things. And we also prayed together; all of the children did. It was not anything forced upon us, it was just something we loved to do, for it made us feel so loved and so cared about. We didn't need each other to do this but it was beautiful when we did share the total experience of our Father's love.

I know not how "long" it was before I heard the cry from that faraway place again, but it came again. "Help Us, help us".

My counselor appeared and together we walked to the building that represented the planet Earth. We stood outside. He took my hand and placed it on where my "heart" was supposed to be. He nodded, and I without him, entered into that building that represented the planet Earth.

(17)

Vivenus: Starchild

At once, it was noisy. I heard sounds that I had never heard before and it was a shock to my aura and the first time, I could not remain long.

There is a city on Venus, we call Cathedral City. The trees are all gold, the leaves a lighter gold and the grass is gold, to deep gold. There are pathways here that are white and flowers that are crimson. The trees are huge and some meet branch to branch, forming arcs under which we kneel to pray. It is here we come to touch directly with our God and have Him touch us. And in our beginning school, there is land set aside that is our Cathedral City not quite as immense but with the same feeling of holiness and there for the same purpose to touch directly with our God.

I went here to little Cathedral City after entering that "planet Earth" building. I knelt to pray, and returned to me, was the quietness of spirit I had come there for. I went then to the play-fields of our school village but I could not join in the games. The quietness of spirit did not leave me. I watched the other children playing, and then in my mind, I saw one of them fall down. I shook the picture away and he was upright again. Then, Panion my friend, the cat, appeared at my side and I knew somehow school was over.

Panion walked with me as I went to find my counselor. Then Panion disappeared, while my counselor and I stepped onto a pale gold staircase. He motioned me up one step. He bowed his head then lifted it high. I did the same. I took his hand and thanked him. He took my other hand and thanked me and then we both thanked God and that was my "graduation" from beginning school on Venus home star.

I sang my way back to my house, my home at home. Panion reappeared, purring beside me.

(18)

Vivenus: Starchild

Carol Ann Rodriguez

CHAPTER TWO

THE VOICE OF DESTINY

DESTINY IS A FRIEND
PLAYING HIDE AND SEEK:
SHE WAITS FOR YOU TO FIND HER
TO LEAD YOU TO THE MOUNTAIN'S PEAK

My home coming was a great celebration. My family rejoiced for me and let me know their pleasure. My mother, without a stove, had "baked" a cake for the occasion and it seemed almost as big as our house. It was white and in the center was a frost-like painting of a world, not ours. It had blues and greens and browns in it. In the center of the cake was a golden torch-unlit.

My papa wrote a song for the occasion and he played it upon our "piano". Rani painted for me a silhouette of a little song bird. Donnelle gave to me a necklace of tiny silver-red hearts with a chain of pink pearls.

We gathered round the piano and we all sang songs of joy and thanksgiving. We sat in the silence for a while and then came the moment to light the torch that was in the center of the cake. With my mind, I saw a blue and lilac flame and the torch was lit. A white dove flew from the flame and soared and soared and soared till I almost could not see it anymore. Then it made its descent and as it did, a voice spoke and it spoke in the Earth language and for some reason I understood the meaning of the words, "Behold, little one, this celebration: thy reason to be is realized now. Thy purpose unveiled. Return to thy eternal service of devotion and love on planet Earth. The cries ye have heard accept as your own. Mission on Earth is granted. You have been there before and you'll go there again. Thy soul needs the victory and the plan of love on the Earth needs thy soul. Behold, little one, this celebration, this moment, realize your destiny."

How can I remember specific conversation? How can I remember God without God to remind me? These words have stayed with me all throughout my mission on the planet Earth. Sometimes, I have nearly "given up" on you, O' Earth, and then, these very words repeat in my being.

The torch stayed lit. And every set of eyes, my parents, my brothers even Panion the cat's seemed to reflect its flame. I bowed to them. They bowed to me. We knelt in prayer, and then our Venusian pastel sky dimmed as if suddenly, we rested.

The torch is still lit at home even "today" and I know this be-cause it is one of the promises we hold dear at home. A torch that is lit in the name of love for a mission in love on the planet Earth, remains lighted until the mission is accomplished.

(20)

Vivenus: Starchild

On the next new "day", I went right away to Cathedral City. It was so much larger than the one at school village and even more glorious. I wandered softly through this golden land. At last I found the trees beckoning to me and I knelt before them. I spoke aloud in the Earth language for the first time and whispered: "Thank you, Father." I felt His hand upon my head and I felt His love fill my heart and I felt His peace all over the universes He created. And I knew then that His plan would succeed and I felt so very blessed to be a part of it.

Further schooling was required for I knew within me, that I would need preparation for a mission on Earth. I attended what would be equivalent to the Earth college. I was not in a child's form any longer. I do not remember when the transformation happened, perhaps when the torch was lit.

There are only three parts to changing form on Venus. There is the infant stage and the child stage and then the adult stage where all adults appear to be in their "twenties". Beyond that, there is no "aging" on Venus.

LOVE DID NOT MAKE ME TO GROW OLD.
LOVE DID NOT MAKE ME TO FALL APART SOMEDAY.
LOVE MADE ME PERFECT - TO LAST FOREVER.

There is no"death" on Venus either. There is a time in a soul's eternal life where he or she graduates to a higher plane of BEING and a higher world of life force; for Venus home star is not the highest achievement of soul.

When the soul makes the ascent he or she simply soars up, unto the newer.Yet,it is an older world.And the planet of Venus holds a great celebration of life, a rejoicing that speeds the wings of the soul's flight and a song of love to follow his or her trail.

One of the first things I learned at my Venus College School Village was that to leave the planet Earth one first had to shed a costume and then make the ascent. And the ascent was not as swift because the planet did not rejoice.

College School Village was separate from beginning school. It was a smaller village but basically the same structures and form. The buildings were fewer and I only entered one; the one that represented the Earth planet.

I had three counselors: one for the soul, one for the Earth, one for my mission. They each were in tune with the pulse beat upon the Earth and they each were in tune with my own. My first lessons were general, the first being to develop my sixth sense (which on Earth is known as ESP). I was given many "hunches" within my mind, surprise to my thoughts and encouraged to act on them instantly. These "hunches" seemed separated from my heart and feelings and that was my first real step into Earth territory: to separate mind and heart ("thought" and feeling)

(21)

Vivenus: Starchild

as two different forces.

I also had to learn to increase my tuning in power to the divine presence. This was fairly simple until my Earth counselor put some object on the path of my mind, blocking my vision and channels. Eventually, I found the concentration needed and I passed this part of the Earth preparation.

My mission counselor taught me the basic rules of Mission:

1. Keep the torch lit within you.

2. Serve the greater love.

3. Seek not personal gain.

4. Be willing to sacrifice.

5. Realize the overall plan.

6. Realize you are but one part.

7. Give thanks.

8. Expect not to see results immediately.

9. Follow the spirit.

10. Give to yourself what you need.

I was taught about appearances, how on Earth, things and people were not always as they appeared.

In the first part, they wear a covering over their souls which is called flesh and as I entered the Earth atmosphere, a flesh covering would be graced upon me. Therefore, what I would see in "people" would not always be representative of who they really were. They advised me to always look deep into the eyes and try to find who lived there.

I was told about the Earth seasons. We have our own but the changes are not in temperatures but in visions. Our "weather" at home, is not "hot" as you've been told by your "scientists". Perhaps to them, to you, to any wearing flesh, it would seem so. But our soul-spirit forms do not feel "cold" or "hot" but only warm or a fresh cool.

I was taught not to go by what I saw but by what I felt by what I saw.

They created "heat": I first felt warm, then hot, then lifeless. They created for me a winter scene. It was pretty but it was so cold and slippery. I felt a chill, something I had never felt and for one slight moment I felt "pain". They created a strong wind much different

(22)

- 22 -

than the gentle breeze at home. I heard its roaring and I felt for one slight moment confused. They showed me a smile that was not a smile and they let me hear the sound of applause.

My soul counselor impressed upon me the need on Earth to follow my feelings all the way through and to follow their course of action. My soul counselor told me that even though I was on a mission of service, that I would not be doing that service on the planet Earth unless my soul had need to grow there. Were there thank you's I had not expressed? Was there forgiveness I had not felt? What was lacking within my soul? At home, I felt no discomfort within. But I was advised that when I reached the Earth plane of consciousness and seeming to be- I would feel the lacks within me.

I was warned that I would not consciously remember any of these preparations and studies once upon planet Earth. It would be a part of my being but not a part of my knowing, not for the role I would be playing.

My Earth counselor taught me about "darkness" on the planet Earth. How subtle it was, how crafty and how it alone was preventing the planet Earth from being a planet of love.

WITHOUT THE LIGHT TO SEE IS A CHOICE
SOME SOULS DO CHOOSE UPON EARTH.
WITHOUT LOVE TO FEEL IS A CHOICE
SOME SOULS DO CHOOSE UPON THE EARTH.
AND THESE SOULS IN THEIR ROLES
ACT OUT THEIR CHOICES.
WHEN THEY LEAVE THE EARTH, THEY MAKE THE CHOICE
AND REMAIN EARTH BOUND.
THEY WANT TO GO ON EXPRESSING THEIR MISERY,
THEIR FEAR. THEY LOOK FOR HOUSES TO ENTER
WHEREIN THEY MAY LIVE AND FIND FURTHER
EXPRESSION. THE HOUSES THEY ENTER ARE
HOUSES OF LIGHT, THAT SOMETIMES FORGET TO
TURN THE LIGHT ON.
THE DARKNESS ON EARTH SEEMS VICTORIOUS
BECAUSE SO MANY SOULS OF LIGHT ARE UNAWARE.

Mission on Earth, to make the Earth like home? Why was it not? Why did souls choose misery? Did not the same Creator who created Venus, create the planet Earth? What was so different that caused souls to make such strange choices? I was answered, though they could tell me, I would not know until I went there and experienced it.

Each of my counselors gave me quizzes and tests to see if I knew what and what not to do in certain Earth situations.

My soul counselor once struck me in the face, not hard, but enough to truly startle me. On Venus, there is no violence, no anger. Her face looked like I had never seen it look. Her eyes were filled with something

(23)

Vivenus: Starchild

a lot less than love, and I felt for the first time a hurt, near tears. I asked her why she struck me. And she struck me again. I got down on my knees and called on our Heavenly Father to help her remove this plague of unlove within her. And then I opened my eyes and she, who was so beautiful, was smiling, and said I had passed the test. And then she said so softly that on Earth, though it may not happen physically, many souls would hurt me, strike me, and the right by love's way to react was to kneel and pray for them.

In College Village we were not always with our counselors, not always "studying". We were allowed to move at our own pace and to digest these things we were learning. I went for many walks in the village and lingered in my introductions to the planet Earth.

During one such just "being-in-it" time, that same voice from the faraway place called to me again. "Help us. help us, help me." Now I did know where it was coming from, and I looked down to the Earth. I walked to the edge of our world of Venus, and tried to see through all the atmospheres. I saw a tiny figure; arms reaching out and up to me. I tuned in or tried to, but no more was I to receive at that moment.

My mission counselor gave me a quiz once: "Is your mission to write a book?" I answered "no." 'Is your mission to be a great speaker for the truth?" I answered "no." "Is your mission to sing your way into the hearts of Earth?" I smiled..."probably not." "Is your mission to become Earth-rich and spend your riches spreading the word?" I answered "no." Is your mission to be carefully plotted out in your mind?" I answered "no". "Is your mission to follow the spirit and let it lead you to accomplishment?" I answered "yes," and I passed the test.

I tasted "coffee" in College Village and Earth type food and earth water. I learned how to speak and how to write and I learned how the Earth tells "time". I learned about "money", though I didn"t understand it, (still don't) and I learned about necessity.

There is nothing and no one we "need" on Venus. Or rather if we do, it is given to us, before we realize we "need" on Venus. Or rather if we do, it is given to us, before we realize we "need" it or him or her.

I spent many dim pastels in College Village, though not as many as when I went to beginning school. We do not count on Venus. We do not measure out existence. We live in the right now, even as we prepare for our tomorrow.

My "graduation" was another thank you time between me and each of my counselors. All of my counselors, even in beginning school, preferred and chose to have no "name". Some of us are that evolved and so united into love, we need no separate identification.

(24)

Vivenus: Starchild

RETURNING HOME - REUNITED SOUL MATES

I returned to my house at Home. There was still more preparation for my going to Earth. I knew I was not yet ready. But it was time to rest from the Earth matters to clear my being and return to the state of grace of perfect love.

I still did not know how I would get to Earth, how I would fit in with Earth, or even really what my specific mission on Earth was. But it was time to put it all away from me. Time to live in and remember who I really was.

It was wonderful to get back to the Venusian way of living and being. Without a care, without a "thought", without an interruption of flow.

There was someone new at our house when I arrived, and yet by my heart, he was not new to me. I felt him as the part of me that was missing, tho I had never consciously missed it, or him. He was the male counter-part to me. We laughed at the same cloud design. We smiled at the same rainbow. He held me with his eyes and I could not break from his embrace. My soul mate, who may or may not be upon this earth plane in this now, but probably is not. Avec is his name.

All souls have their counter-parts. No soul is born without its other half. We bring out the tenderness of love in each other and no other soul but our other half can do the job. Avec walked with me and always brought me back to our house when the skies grew dim. He shared with me a part of myself and I shared him with him. We changed into two other forms for "fun" and swam as two little fish in a stream. We climbed a rainbow and with our minds, built a little house on top of it and we pictured ourselves in that house when we would be ready to share the adventure. We saw ourselves in Cathedral City, but we did not go there. For if we had, God, our Father, would have "married" us. When two go as one in Cathedral City, it is for this purpose of unity.

The physical expressions of love on Venus is minimal. We embrace, we do not kiss. And we do not ever blend as one unless the Father sanctions it. And He does not sanction it until soul mates want to share in the life experience of parenthood. Avec and I were not ready for this.

SOUL MATES, AS ONE IN THEIR BEGINNING
DISCONNECTED AFTER A TIME,
ALLOWED AS SEPARATE ENTITIES AND EXPRESSIONS
TO EXPLORE THE UNIVERSE OF BEING.
WE CLIMB THE STARS, SEPARATELY
WE CLIMB THE STARS AS ONE.
SOUL MATES, APART, REUNITED,
APART, REUNITED, UNTIL
THE BLEND IS FOREVER ONE.

(25)

Vivenus: Starchild

Avec stayed with me but for a little while. He had to return to his journey of soul, as I had to return to mine.

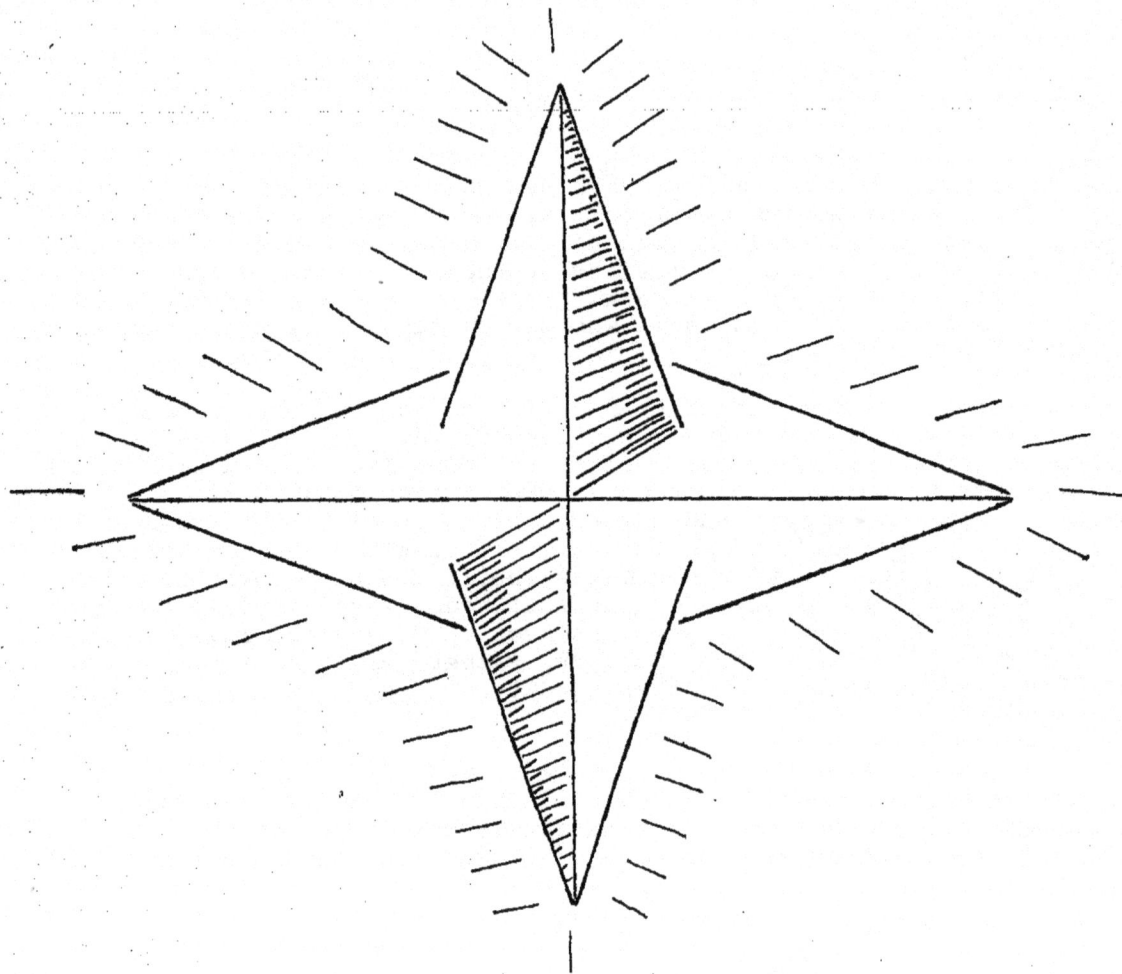

CHAPTER THREE

TWIN SOUL OF EARTH

An Earth identity had been chosen for me, but not by anyone on Venus, but by a soul living upon the Earth. The cries I heard that reached my heart were meant for me. The soul that I am, without the blend of my soul mate, is still of two parts. One high, one low, one bold, one meek. Twin souls, identical in looks, but not necessarily identical in expression.

My twin soul was the voice of the cries I heard. She had agreed to play a role on Earth and hoped that through it, she could make the Earth a better place, a place of love.

Perhaps because I knew the Earth language now, I was able to tune in to her and speak to her. I pictured the Earth planet and I prayed to see and be where she was standing. Narrow streets, little cars with big voices, so many sounds, no silence anywhere. I called a quiet loud to find her and lift her up in her soul to our land. It was "night-time" upon the Earth and her flesh was sleeping.

We laughed when we first saw each other. It was like looking into the lake. We spoke a little, not of Earth but of home. I walked in silence with her, around our world, and then she returned to Earth, for it was time for her to get up in the morning. She told me nothing of her role on Earth nor why she wanted out- not then. She could only speak of her sorrow while she was in her sorrow. I had to tune in to her while she was on the Earth, and "awake" and conscious.

She told me that missions must not be called "missions" on Earth, that they must be called "dreams", and dreams - like wishes, may or may not come true. She told me the Earth laughs at those who dream a dream, admires determination, but ridiucles it.

She told me too, that feeling souls, had difficulty surviving on planet Earth, for the people were embarrassed or frightened by too much feeling. She said her only help in all her years was that she sang. It helped her to express feelings and the people did not silence her when she sang. She said she had hoped that her mission called dream on Earth would be to be able to sing love to the Earth people and lift them out of their indifference to life and caring. But in her pursuit she felt nothing but pain and hurt. And in her pursuit the rejection was too great to bear.

She was the youngest child of five children, born into a wealthy (earth-wise) family. Living in a huge, huge house with servants to run it and to watch over the children whose parents were never there. One servant, a governess, used to beat her, lock her in a closet, force her to eat and then force her to eat that which she could not keep down. Her two older sisters (next in line in age) also lived in games of cruelty in their own ways. A piece of candy was held from a string

(27)

Vivenus: Starchild

from a second floor window, the three little girls jumped for their
"reward". After a long time of this "game", a basket of candy would
be thrown. A record was put on the victrola, the song "Red Rose"
played loud and my twin soul, from the age of five to eight, would
be beaten at the whim of the darkness. A chauffeur was there who tried
to help the little girls but perhaps he was afraid of the darkness
too. His name was Herman and he was as close to being a parent as
the three little girls had in their beginning years. They had a dog,
lots of cats, a canary and each other.

My twin soul was the age of eight when her Earth mother left
the Earth. Then the dad fired the governess, wrote a list of rules,
and tried to be a parent. He re-married and the step-mother was
possessed by the drinker.

At the age of eleven, my twin soul was taken to the Palace
Theatre in New York City, to see Judy Garland on stage. And it was
then she decided that that was what she wanted to do, to cry and not
be beaten for it, but instead, loved. To sing, to laugh, to be free
expressing her feelings and not to be punished for it, but loved all
the more.

In school, she performed in all the plays. There, by the applause,
she received the love and praise and appreciation she so longed for.

She was determined all her childhood to be a famous singing
star, simply that she could love freely and be loved and through all
that love, perhaps help her world be lifted a little more into the
light.

She "ran away" from college at the age of twenty, from Florida,
in the midst of a hurricane and somehow, got to New York City,
"where dreams come true."

She told me she began contacting me when she was a child. I did
not tune in to her until she was an adult in New York City.

> O' CHILD, ON EARTH
> THE ROLE YOU CHOSE
> WHY DID YOU CHOOSE SOMETHING
> SO MUCH WITH PAIN?
> WHY DID YOU NOT
> ASK LOVE FOR LOVE
> SO YOU WOULD NOT
> HAVE TO COME BACK AGAIN?

My twin soul's name was Viv - like mine - except that hers was
an abbreviation. She believed somehow that I could fulfill her dream
for her and that somehow, she would be able to feel that as herself.
I did not know if that was the plan, but I did know that singing was
the tool I would use to reach the Earth. I remember promising her
that I would sing for her and live her dream as though it were mine

(28)

Vivenus: Starchild

and that through that, I would accomplish my mission on Earth.

All of this in one's consciousness does not make for a happy
vibration. And happiness is a must on Venus, a rule of the land.
Though these conversations between my twin soul and I were erased
when they were done, they were I knew, growing within my being and
I could feel that my journey to Earth would be soon.

<u>INNER REFLECTION</u>

The torch that was lit for me glowed brighter. I used to sit
and look into it for long, long times and sessions.

The next time I entered Cathedral City was for the Invocation.
I knelt, and the Father talked with me, a conversation wherein I could
ask Him questions pertaining to my mission on Earth and He would
answer. I was told that the part I would play in the drama on Earth
was that so I could become as Earth, even of Earth, for a time that
what had happened within each one upon the Earth, would happen thus
to me. I asked Him what had happened? He answered that I would find
out. And He promised that when that darkest moment came upon my soul,
that He would be there to rush me through the tunnel back to the
light but He said that just as all His children on Earth to whom He
also made this promise, that I would not remember enough to count on
His help to be there. But that was part of the plan and I would understand in time.

At home, we each are so very close to God, our Father and there
is no thing and no one who comes before a private moment with Him.
We are trained to hear Him the instant He calls to us. And I could
not, while I was home, imagine any moment in eternity without this
close, close feeling but He warned me that it would happen, that I
would seem to "lose" Him, then feel as though He had forsaken me.
And while I would never forget where I had come from, it somehow
would seem meaningless.

"...Lighten the Earth planet with love..." Those were His words,
clarifying my mission. He said it three times, "Lighten the Earth
planet with love...", "Lighten the Earth planet with love...",
"Lighten the Earth planet with love..."

   ...LOVE IS GREATER THAN THE GREATEST IDEA;
     LOVE IS WISER THAN THE MOST BRILLIANT THOUGHT;
     LOVE IS BETTER THAN PROVING THYSELF RIGHT;
     LOVE IS STRONGER AND SHALL CONQUER THE NIGHT.

"...TO LIGHTEN THE EARTH PLANET WITH LOVE ..."
   ...DO NOT BECOME DISENCHANTED FOR TOO LONG.
   DO NOT BECOME ENCHANTED BY THOSE
   ENCHANTED WITH YOU.
   SEEK NO PROFIT BUT TO THY SOUL

(29)

Vivenus: Starchild

```
AND REMEMBER - REMEMBER
IT IS BUT A ROLE.

NO MATTER WHAT COMES TO YOU
NO MATTER WHAT IS OFFERED YOU
DO NOT TIRE FROM YOUR TASK
AND LIGHTEN THE EARTH PLANET WITH LOVE..."
```

I returned to my house and to my "immediate" family. We stayed very close to one another. I did not know if they knew any details of my mission on Earth. It might be they knew more than I. We did not "discuss" my journey of soul that was before me. They knew it was not their place to "say a word" about it. They were happy for me, and I was happy for me, too. And though I had been told many things about the Earth, I still could feel that only victory and joy would be with me there.

At home, I was given the complete plan; on Earth, I was given to forget it. So it is with you. If you or I could remember what we agreed upon in Heaven for our roles on Earth, then we would be living on the Earth plane simply by the mind and we would not accomplish the purpose of our soul's progress which is ruled by the heart.

I think I need to forgive but I need to feel forgiveness. I think I need to find peace but I need to feel peace within me.

I know I should be grateful but I need to feel the thank you. Only through the drama can the actor become the part.

One more time, the girl I would be replacing, appeared to me at home. "I hope it is not long. I hope you really will take over for me. I feel that if you will, God will forgive me for what I have to do. And I really have to do it. I cannot bear this cold indifferent world. I can not bear not being allowed the expression of love and loving. And I cannot bear the world of people I care about, not caring about each other and yes, me. Perhaps I was too injured as a child. Perhaps I asked for more than I can handle. Singing is a great healing tonic, but I cannot sing all the hours I am awake. I have a dream but I am afraid it will just take too long to realize it and have it come true. And I know what lies in between to get to the top of my mountain. I cannot and will not play the games of Earth. Please come quickly. Take my place. Sing my song and help God help this Godless world."

I answered her as gently as I could to please be patient, that love's perfect time for the transfer would come. I heard her whisper "Thank You, God" and then there was no other contact with my twin soul while I was yet at home.

On Venus, there is no sadness, no heaviness of spirit, and the information of feelings I received about this girl while I was home, did not "upset" me. She had chosen her role for her soul's reasons and the interchange we would make was in the designs of love's plan

(30)

even as we were born. God knew before we knew, what would happen.
Her release would be soon, and her torment would be no more.

CHAPTER FOUR

A WORLD OF LOVE

```
VENUS HOME STAR
WORLD OF LIGHT
WORLD OF PEACE
WORLD OF BEINGS
ONE WITH THE SPIRIT OF BEAUTY
ONE WITH THE SPIRIT OF TRUTH
ONE WITH THE SPIRIT OF LOVE.
```

No yesterday. No tomorrow. Only now, right now. No sadness. No sorrow. Only joy, just joy.

This is home. This is Venus. A world wherein every life form is as love first made it. Beings flowing in their feelings that they live in the state of love.

Light, no darkness anywhere. Not a doubt. Not a fear. Not a lie. Not a deception. No one pretending to be more than he is not. No one feeling less than she is. No having to "prove" his worth. No having to survive an existence. No having to "earn" one's space.

All equal. No one poor. All rich. No misfits, for each soul is unique and one of a kind. No heroes to worship. No leaders to follow. No newscasters announcing bad news.

No doctors. No sickness. No policemen. No crimes. No prejudice. All colors. No laws but love.

No preachers. All Godly. No religions. Just truth.

```
BEAUTY AND CARING AND LOVING AND LIGHT.
NO STRANGERS, ALL FAMILY.
AND NEVER THE NIGHT.
```

The reality of a light world touches the Earth mind with surprise but the heart feels comforted. For the heart knows what the mind is afraid to believe. The heart on Earth knows because it remembers.

Is it so strange that I am from another world? Where were you before you came to the planet Earth? Did you not exist? Then will you not exist when you leave here?

Love's plan is the circle, not a block of wood. Love reaches out, not slashes down. Love gives, love does not take back.

Love has set forth a plan to teach its young how to fly. They may fly as high and as far and as long as they wish and love is assured that her young will return to the nest.

Vivenus: Starchild

When love creates love, it does not create it with any "mistakes" or flaws. What love makes is perfect. Love made you and love made me; why then do we not seem perfect? Because we left the nest for too long and forgot where we belonged.

The world of Venus has returned to the nest. All of us upon it agree there is no greater love than the love of "God". And we know exactly where to find that love and we go there often. It is within us, within each of us.

Our minds are not exploring what our hearts have no interest in. Our thoughts do not precede our feelings, but follow them.

The mind was given for creative things to make or break or develop ideas. The heart was given only to love. On Venus, there are no divided houses. We are unified beings. There is nothing within any soul that contradicts itself. There is no thought that can inhibit expression of self. There is no one that can delay any one's journey. There are no outer elements to alternate our paths. There is nothing outside of us that concerns us. If we have been brought to the planet Earth, it is because the planet Earth has by love, reached our inner beings.

The planet Venus is, a planet of live, living souls with forms that cannot be seen by the Earth's physical eyes, must not be seen by the planet that would to "claim" it and make it like unto itself.

The Father and His higher angels protect our world of Venus. They form cloud-like vapors over us in those times those on Earth try to "probe". We know when this is being done and we know why. We are not afraid of the Earthlings for our world but perhaps for their own. It is why some of us have volunteered to serve here. We have no desire to claim your world, O' Earth. We only pray that by our visit, you will claim love.

Love, that knows no boundaries. Love, that seeks not, strives not, asks not. Love, that just is. Love, that knows no thing called "fear", no thing called "doubt", no thing called "bad".

Love, that sees love, a perfect state of grace and all it sees, it sees as love would see, as the Creator created it, perfect, finished, complete.

If we reach outside ourselves out of curiosity for a love greater than what is within us, we will reach further and further and move further from the source, who is God.

And so every world was born in a different moment in eternity. And the souls upon the worlds were born in two different moments in eternity. If your understanding is deeper in your heart than your neighbor's then your soul might have been born first on Earth or perhaps second on Venus. You stand on a stairway; your neighbor stands on a

(33)

1960—LAST PHOTO OF GIRL FROM EARTH

1961 – FIRST PHOTO OF VIVENUS ON EARTH

stairway. The Earth stands on a stairway; Venus stands on a stairway - each one on its own step - leading up to the perfection of love, leading back to the source of light everlasting.

How can I describe Venus without describing love? For love is really all there is on Venus and whatever can be seen with our eyes, or touched by our hands, is there by the laws of love.

Love gives gifts bountifully to all its children. The Earth has not opened theirs yet. Venus has.

We are governed by the law of love. We have no presidents, no kings, no one, in charge of all of us. We sail our own ships and we find our own seas. Love's law is based on the circle; what is sent out, returns, in thought, in "word" or expression, in deed. It is a law. It cannot be broken. Even the Earth who chooses slumber and not to awake to the law of love, finds the law infallible. What is being sent forth into the Earth atmosphere returns to the life expression that sent it.

So it is with Venus. But we send nothing forth but love. We expect the best, are aware of nothing else and so we receive the best.

We flow in feelings. We have no words. We see what love would have us see and the divine pictures in our minds are given us, we do not force to come.

THE FOUNDATION OF VENUS

Venus is made up of not nations divided, but small villages wherein one can find another expression of him or herself. There is a kind of a mayor of each village who welcomes the souls that enter it. That is basically his or her main function, though he or she also calls us to gather at times for the prayer of Thanksgiving. The mayor of the village is not "elected" but chosen because he or she has volunteered. This is his or her service to love and his or her mission on the planet Venus.
The light on Venus, there is no sun. There is no moon. We see no "stars" when evening comes. Yet, through each life created, from the blade of white grass, to the silver branch of the silver tree, every leaf, every animal, every being, each glows its own light. It is a God-light and there is no other way to "explain" it.

God is the light. And when He lives in us and through us, He can't help but to glow and radiate His glory.

We do not need to "sleep". We do not get "tired". We rest in love in our twilight of evening.

There is much to "do" on Venus but we don't always have to be doing. For you see, we are busy "being".

(36)

Vivenus: Starchild

There is no boredom on Venus, no restlessness, no "waiting". When we ask, it is given. We ask in the name of love, we give thanks, we make ourselves ready to receive and it is brought to us.

The colors I've described in the previous pages of my home-land are as near as I could come in words, to what they really are. They are vivid yet so gentle. There is nothing harsh. And with all the light that glows through all the life and living colors, there is never any glare. Perhaps it is the blending of all the colors that makes Venus look like a wonderland just as the Earth sometimes notices what happens to their planet come the season of autumn. The fairyland of colors that magically happens to some of the Earth planet.

We have no electricity. We have no need of an artificial light. We use candles sometimes but they do not melt away.

You have human rights on Earth; we have divine rights on Venus: to be free in spirit, thought and heart. To be silent to listen to love, to grow in love's time by love's grace, to follow the spirit of destiny, to be true to thine own self, to learn from every form of life something of divine love, to love all life created by love, to be good to thyself, to thy family, to the friends, to ask permission of only one, the Creator, to be blessed in the kingdom of eternal love.

The only roles played on Venus are "parent", "child", "counselor", and "mayor". These are the only "identities". But no images are created and no illusions drawn. We have no expectations of one another.

"Marriage" on Venus come to soul mates only, and comes only if the souls want to renew the oneness of spirit. There is nothing on Venus to "work out" with one another. All souls there, have made their peace with one another. Female souls who choose to parent, blend with their male counterpart. There is no pain, no discomfort and the child is "born" where it was conceived, in Cathedral City. The planet holds a celebration. The child newly born on Venus is also a brand "new" soul on Venus and so other births transpire at the same moment in eternity and there is joy throughout our land.

Venus is seemingly a planet of withouts. We don't have money; we don't have wars; we don't have "jobs"; we don't have cars; we don't have bombs; we don't have guns; we don't have pain; we don't have lonely; we don't have misunderstood; we don't have ridicule; we don't have the unfortunate. We don't have a lot that the Earth has, and there is no lack anywhere.

What love has made is real. What love has not made, does not exist. And that is how Venusians live. It is truth, not a wish, and yet, if you only wish it, it is not true. Love did not make fear, so fear does not exist. Love does not get angry because love has been there and understands.

Things are created by thoughts but the thoughts on Venus agree with

(37)

the heart and thus no thing outside of reality touches us.

Venusian "food" is not a necessity, but a sometimes treat. In times of celebration, we enjoy it. What is eaten is either grown from sacred ground or created by someone's thought. We have no stoves, no pots or pans.

We do not use love's gifts to us; we enjoy them. The ponies are never ridden and the flowers are never picked. The trees are never sawed down and should we want to paint a picture, a fabric is created for that purpose.

We do not have streets or roads on Venus but there are paths of gold or white leading to here, to there, to nowhere in particular. Some paths have flowers beside them and these are the paths that lead to our rainbows. Our rainbows have many, many stripes of colors. We can touch our rainbows, even stand or sit upon them and share in the glory of our universe.

The clothes we wear vary, according to the individual. The coloring of our hair, our eyes is according to our soul's design. Not all "angels" are blue-eyed and blonde, and not all angels wear long white robes.

To describe on paper, in words, and by this, attempt to paint a picture of a sacred world, feels almost to me to desecrate it. I pray you will understand that what I share of Venus Home Star is but a bare touch of its reality. Reality on Venus is reality anywhere; that which will last beyond "time". And there is nothing that will last beyond "time" but love.

> VENUS HOME STAR
> OH, PERFECT WORLD THAT LOVE CREATED
> TELL ME YOU ARE STILL THERE.
> TELL ME THAT MY LONGING FOR YOU
> IS BUT BEING THERE.
> VENUS HOME STAR
> I BRING THEE DOWN FOR A MOMENT TO THOSE ON EARTH
> WHO ALSO MISS YOU - LONG FOR YOU
> AND WHO HOPE THAT WHAT THEY REMEMBER
> IS NOT AN ILLUSION BUT THE REALITY OF LIFE.
> I BRING THEE DOWN FOR THOSE ON EARTH
> TO BE GIVEN COURAGE OF THEIR FEELINGS
> AND CONVICTION OF THEIR KNOWING
> AND COMMITMENT TO THEIR DREAM.
> VENUS HOME STAR, I BRING THEE DOWN TO EARTH
> THAT THE EARTH MAY BE LIFTED UP.

(38)

CHAPTER FIVE

THE SWOOPS

Spaceships, I call them "swoops" because I'm a Venusian. And Venusians, if they name a thing, name it for what it does rather than for how it looks. A spaceship does swoop, as a bird swoops, silently.

The swoops on Venus are all colors and all sizes and many shapes. There are several giant swoops that carry many smaller ones inside, to let them disembark over the lands they must keep vigil.

At home, there is a special part of our land to house our swoops. We do not have need of them on our world but only to other worlds, especially to the planet Earth.

There are many on Earth who have seen and many who felt pure love from the experience. And that is the way it should be.

We are here to help lift the Earth to light. We are not here to add to the fear that already permeates the Earth's atmosphere, the fear that keepeth away perfect love.

There are imposters flying your skies, O'Earth. There are objects made to look as our ships look. And there are even entities trying to masquerade as us.

Be not fooled. And be not frightened. They cannot harm you, not who you really are. At best, at worst, they can only delay you from trusting us, we who love you and who come to help.

Who are these imposters? They are not from any other world but your own, O' Earth. They are from your atmosphere. They are not physical beings but souls who deliberately seek to cause mischief and havoc on your planet. And they are allowed to continue their folly until they see the light.

This is darkness, some of which manifests into what seems real objects, even real "people", but it is the craft of the darkness to make its illusions seem real.

So it is with your emotions, O' Earth. What you feel and cannot stop feeling and do not like feeling, may not be you at all. And your thoughts, the voices inside your mind, reminding you of despair and sorrow and pain and hopelessness. These thoughts may not even be you. Trying to "get over" an experience and somehow you can't stop "thinking" about it. And so you do things to make you forget, things painful to your soul - so painful it leaves you, leaving an empty house, wherein, a soul lost in darkness, can enter and live and find his or her expression of misery can prevail.

(39)

Vivenus: Starchild

It is this darkness that is sending up the clouds of smoke from planet Earth. It is this darkness that seems to be destroying the planet and many souls who try to live upon the planet. And it is for this reason that swoops hover over your skies.

What do you do too much of, that you secretly wish you didn't do? Why can't you stop? Are you not in charge of your ship? Who has taken over your house and made it theirs? Who do you want to represent, the light? Or the darkness?

This book may never reach your hands. Most of my works in these twenty-one years have not. I know not who stops it, whether it is the darkness or it is the plan. Herein, is the truth to set you free from your "moods". Herein, is the awareness you need to combat the darkness.

The swoops in your skies can make themselves visible or invisible. They are piloted by two usually male souls. They are trained their whole life time to maneuver these swoops. They know how to form clouds around themselves. They know how to instantly appear and instantly disappear. And the swoops that are in your skies, O' Earth, are there on a mission of love: to polarize with light the negativity that is in the Earth atmosphere.

So much fear, so much doubt, so much gloom and despair floods your skies with a volatile chemical - dangerous. And were my space brothers not in their swoops above you, what havoc that is on the Earth would reach the heavens. Your earthquakes and volcanoes and floods and hurricanes and intensities of seasons and disasters upon disasters are the results of the darkness. The darkness has claimed so many minds on the Earth, that the hearts are not able to function. Awareness is a light. And with a light there is no darkness.

The swoops in the sky not only block what is rising from the Earth but also ray down light in crucial places to protect your planet from complete self-destruction.

We bide our time, while love allows the children on Earth to find their way back to the light. It is strange: though the darkness is the enemy on Earth, it also speeds those of light to the arms of love, of God.

My mission is not spaceships, not swoops and I do not know as much about their workings as you would like me to know. And if I did, I am confident that I would not be allowed or given permission to reveal all. The Earth has a way of misusing the gifts of love, using what is of love for a wrong purpose. I know you will understand why perhaps my knowledge of swoops is limited only to my own personal experience and observation.

Vivenus: Starchild

INSIDE THE SHIP

The swoop I travelled in, to journey to planet Earth from Venus, was silver inside and out. Shaped like a bell and about as large as a small bungalow. A swoop needs no fuel, no water and has no parts that will break.

In flight, you feel no motion, no motion at all. And yet, as you look through the little windows, you see the colors of the changing atmospheres and you know you are enroute. Swoops make no sound and they do not leave ground like a rocket. There is no force but love, it is like a magnet that directs the flight.

Inside the swoop I travelled, were two decks, an upper room and lower room and on each of the eight wallings. There is what resembles a steering wheel in the lower cabin and instead of turning it around, it is pulled first up then down. There is what looks like a gear stick-shift and this seems to be what actually steers the swoop, for instead of going up and down, it moves in a circle.

There is a pedal for lowering, a pedal for gradual ascend, a pedal for hovering, a pedal for quick flight, a pedal for gradual descend and a switch for continuous and steady flight. There is what looks like a large compass and there is a button for various colored lights for the outside to ray.

In a swoop, one must wear a space suit. Some are silver, some are white or pale blue. They are soft and comfortable and made of a substance resistant to grounding. They are also insulated for warmth.

When a swoop returns from a mission, it is serviced. It is a service of cleansing and purifying.

The spaceships, swoops are the transportation of all worlds but one. From world to world some soar. God made every star and there are souls who would to explore every one.

There are people on Earth who have kept their minds open to every aspect of my life I have to this date shared and then when they hear of the way I arrived here, the door to their minds, shuts. If they "like" me, they will try to translate my events into something they can live with in their minds. But when it comes to the part about the space travel, on a real space ship, there is no way they can interpret that into their own language.

(41)

Vivenus: Starchild

<u>FOR THOSE WHO BELIEVE</u>

What I have and am sharing in this book, I have not shared before except in essence and briefly. I am surprised that I am able to share this much. I am surprised that I am able to find words to communicate a wordless existence. If this book turns out not to be detailed enough, if you wish it were "longer", forgive that I can only give what I am given to give. And though I was asked years ago on planet Earth, to do what I am doing now, it is only now that love has sanctioned it.

Is now the time that you are ready? Is now the time that I am ready? Or is this too....to be put aside until after I am gone? Love knows. And I rejoice in love who knows what is best for its plan for you, O'Earth.

Spaceships..swoops, do not fear them. They are your friends. Without them, O' Earth, you would not still be an Earth.

If you who read this, have witnessed one of our swoops in your skies, know now you were deliberately selected to see. A special mission awaits you if you will not fear what is not real. If you who read this, have not seen, but want to, know now: a special mission awaits you, too. And if you who read this don't care about swoops at all, but only to make your world a better place: tune in to your assignment. Perhaps now is the time when all shall be revealed. Perhaps now is the time, those who believe will not shut out those who do not.

There are children of light who believe with all their hearts that they have to "succeed" in this world and thus they have no "time" to pursue the dreamings in their hearts. Do not shun them though they may laugh at you. They are love's children trying to help their world by more love but only in the ways the Earth says they can.

They must be awakened for they shall be a great strength to us.

> A SWOOP IS A GLORIOUS WAY TO FLY
> THE SPEED OF WINGS
> THE SILENCE OF THE BIRD WHO GLIDES.
> THE QUICK DEPARTURE
> THE SAFE DESCEND.
> A THING OF BEAUTY
> OF DIGNITY, OF GRACE.
> A SWOOP IS THE FRIEND
> OF THE SPACE TRAVELER
> A CARRIER OF JUSTICE
> AND TRUTH
> ON WINGS OF LOVE.

(42)

Vivenus: Starchild

THE SHARING OF IMPORTANT MOMENTS

Venus, Home Star. What I share of my homeland is revealed of my soul. This task is a painful experience for me. For I feel an invasion of privacy. I make it all sound so casual. I put it into Earthly conversation and as I write, it grates my soul. I share not everything, I could not. I would not. But I pray it is enough to stir your memories to shake away this nightmare we live on the Earth plane that you will realize it is but a dream, a very bad dream from which ye shall be awakened.

Love shall awake you, love on Earth as it is in Heaven.

When I was a child (way before I was aware of my mission on Earth) there was a game I would play with my special friend, Anna. We would create a fabric and blindfold one another. Then we would try to see if we could see without seeing. I would try to lead her to her house; and she would try to lead me to mine. The game would sometimes last until the sky began to dim its pastel pink, and we'd have to remove the blindfolds and return to our families to rest till dawn. But when we would succeed in seeing without seeing and reach our destinations by the invisible paths, we would make "crowns" for each other and place them on our heads. And we would feel such great joy to know victory.

I sang a lot as a child, songs without words. Many times I could be found sitting on a limb of a silver tree next to a little red bird or yellow bird and we would sing together - ever since the little deep blue and white songbird taught me how. My parents sometimes thought me home, but I was too full with being as a bird to tune in to them. So they would have to appear in form.

Childhood on Venus is a time to increase the "thank you" in us.

Before I journeyed to the planet Earth on my mission, a kind of a celebration was held for me by many of my friends on our land of love. These friends had just returned from Earth and though they didn't communicate details of their individual missions there, just by their presence, I somehow felt more assurance of the task ahead. It was a banquet and was held outside in the flowered fields of home.

One girl soul took a picture of all of us with no camera. And there we were on a huge pale yellow fabric, all of us nearly as large as we really were. And I was promised she would take another picture on my return from Earth to see if any change had happened in my soul or theirs, in the time I would not be there.

I went back to my house, lifted up my torch and set it down. Then I walked to Cathedral City. I knelt, and for the longest time I felt only the quiet. For the first time at home, I felt like I was "waiting". Then He appeared. The one the Earth knows as "Jesus". He is the Father when the Father wants to appear to us when He wants us to feel strongly His friendship. I did not speak. And He only smiled.

(43)

Vivenus: Starchild

Vivenus: Starchild

It was a smile that carressed my being: "lighten the Earth planet with love." He held a crown in His hand, a crown so gloriously arrayed in jewels of sapphire and rubies and white pearls. The crowns that my friend Anna and I had made seemed as paper mache to this that He held. "You will return to this, and remember always, I am with thee."

Then He made manifest my torch and re-ignited the flame and set the crown above it. Through the flame and through the crown again flew the little white dove. But this time it soared and soared and soared and did not descend again.

Then He was not there anymore, who the Earth knows as "Jesus", Prince of Love.

His appearance to me, a gift of ultra love, but I was not the only one to whom He ever appeared. For any on Venus who have need of His right-there presence, ask and He comes. I do not consciously remember asking but I do know that missions on Earth need this blessing above all blessings for us to carry on.

MY JOURNEY TO EARTH

I felt so high, almost dizzy, so full almost to burst with love. I felt so much joy, my eyes spilled with tears as I walked to the part of our land that sheltered my swoop.

I knew it was mine. It rayed its light to me. I boarded it and waited for my pilots. As I waited, I became familiar with this new shelter I would have for what I learned later would be Earth "time", six "weeks" in the Earth year 1960, it was more than just a matter of holding information in my mind; I had to, in this time, make the other girl's memories my own. Her feelings had to become mine. Her thoughts, her way of speech and the things that brought her laughter. Whatever she was, I had to be. My mission, part one, was that I had to be of the Earth until I could be of the Earth no more.

There was a light mist in the swoop and a subtle perfumed scent. It felt warm and cozy and I sat down on the pale green bench. It was soft and comfortable. I saw a silver-white suit hanging in the air without a hanger. I knew it was for me. I went to touch it and instantly it was on me. So were the silver canvas-like shoes.

I felt different in that suit, taller and stronger but I knew my form had not changed, only my feelings for the journey ahead.

I knelt which I also did before I entered my swoop. And delight to my heart, my pilots entered: my two Venusian "immediate family" brothers: Rani and Donnelle.

They joined me in prayer and then we took hands and became one in our mission for Earth. We embraced and then we "got down to business".

(45)

Vivenus: Starchild

They told me to rest. I did. I thought they did too, but when I opened my eyes, I saw the sky moving, the colors changing from pink, to white, to yellow, to lilac, to blue. I sat in the quiet of the beauty and the stillness of the gentle light for quite some time. Then I tuned in to my brothers, first one, then the other, but they would not respond. They spoke: "from here on in, you must be as you will be on Earth. No Venusian advantages. We must not tune in to one another. When we wish to communicate, we must speak in Earth words."

And so we began my beginning in being an Earthling. I made many mistakes, pronounced words wrong and tuned in when I should have spoken. I learned some Earth songs that my twin soul was singing. I learned about aging on Earth and how time was measured on Earth and about many aspects of the Earth physical plane that would not have registered in me, had I tried to absorb it at home.

"The girl you will be replacing on Earth is the "age" of twenty years old. Therefore, the only change that will happen in your presence is that by the atmospheres of light your soul form will thicken, grow dense and become as flesh. Your are her physical double and your looks even now are very near to identical. It is the plan that all life has its physical double, some where, some world, maybe even one's own.

You will have no difficulty in convincing those on Earth you are her. And it is made easier as she is a stranger herself in the city she has chosen for this transfer.

The city you will enter and live upon for a time on the Earth is called "New York". It is one of the largest cities upon the Earth. It is crowded with people, with noise, with many vibrations of light and dark. It is the city on Earth where many go to make their dreams come true. It is a "dangerous" city on the physical plane but no harm will come to you. We hope you will remember that."

Hope. What was that? We had none of that at home. Hope?

    HOPE
    WHEN YE HAVE NOT THE FAITH OF WHO YOU ARE
    AND WHAT YOU WANT.
    HOPE
    THE BEGINNING TO A TORCH UNLIT
    THE WICK OF THE CANDLE.
    HOPE
    A TINY SPARK WITHIN THE HEART
    LONGING TO IGNITE
    THE WINGS OF THE BIRD
    WHO HAS NOT YET TRIED THEM.
    HOPE
    IT IS ALL THE EARTH PEOPLE HAVE LEFT.

(46)

Vivenus: Starchild

REPLACING MY TWIN SOUL

My brothers handed me a dress; red and black, straight skirt. They also handed me a pair of black high heel shoes. I went to the upper room of our swoop and changed clothes as an Earthling wiggling and squirming, buttoning and unbuttoning and trying to maneuver in these strange earth shoes. I put my spacesuit back on over the Earth costume.

I was given the address and told how I would get there (on foot) to the hotel room where my twin soul had been staying. I was given $150 dollars as that was the amount she had left. I was then given a long lecture about how important to the Earthlings was money. They did things not from the heart, simply to attain it, for without it, they did not think they could survive. They said it would be even harder for me than for the girl I was replacing, to adjust to the Earth way of forgetting what you love to do and do what you have to do. They said most Earth people adjusted but that I probably never would. They were right.

The girl I was to replace didn't play games so I didn't have to learn any. She was sincere and honest and wanting so much to be of help to people. She was intense about her dream and I had to find within me that intensity of spirit, lining it up, about a song instead of about life. This girl was proud, I had to learn pride.

Much was explained to me in those six weeks in space and more and more I was changing by the magic of love to this other person. My brothers' looks did not change but I could see in their eyes, that I was making the transformation.

The closer we drew to the Earth, the more I took on the role. I became less communicative, more private with what I was feeling and more withdrawn. Once in a while I would sing my brothers a song, for suddenly I knew many Earth songs.

And then I heard her voice.

"Yes, it is time. Right now. Right here. I leave not life but only the Earth pretense at it. I leave with hope that my path will soar me above the clouds that smother me. I leave with hope someone will come from a better world and do what I cannot.

I pray dear God, forgive me. I pray, dear God, to let me go to a place where dreams come true. No one will miss me here except You, God. But You do not need me. For I am not strong enough to do it. Send help to me. Take me up. Send help to Earth."

My swoop lowered and lowered in an instant. And I could see nothing through the little windows. I stepped from my space suit, and heaved a sigh. My brothers bowed their heads. I walked from the swoop, out the doorway, then jumped a little distance onto the Earth.

(47)

Vivenus: Starchild

It was autumn in New York. The air was cool. The sky was dark. The ground was hard. It was Central Park, isolated, night time - 10 PM, September 24, 1960.

My swoop hovered. I saw my brothers' hands reach out on the other side of the swoop from which I came. Then my sight was blocked.

The cloud around the swoop thickened ever more. And silently, quickly, it soared into the sky, blinking its lights to bid me love's blessings of peace.

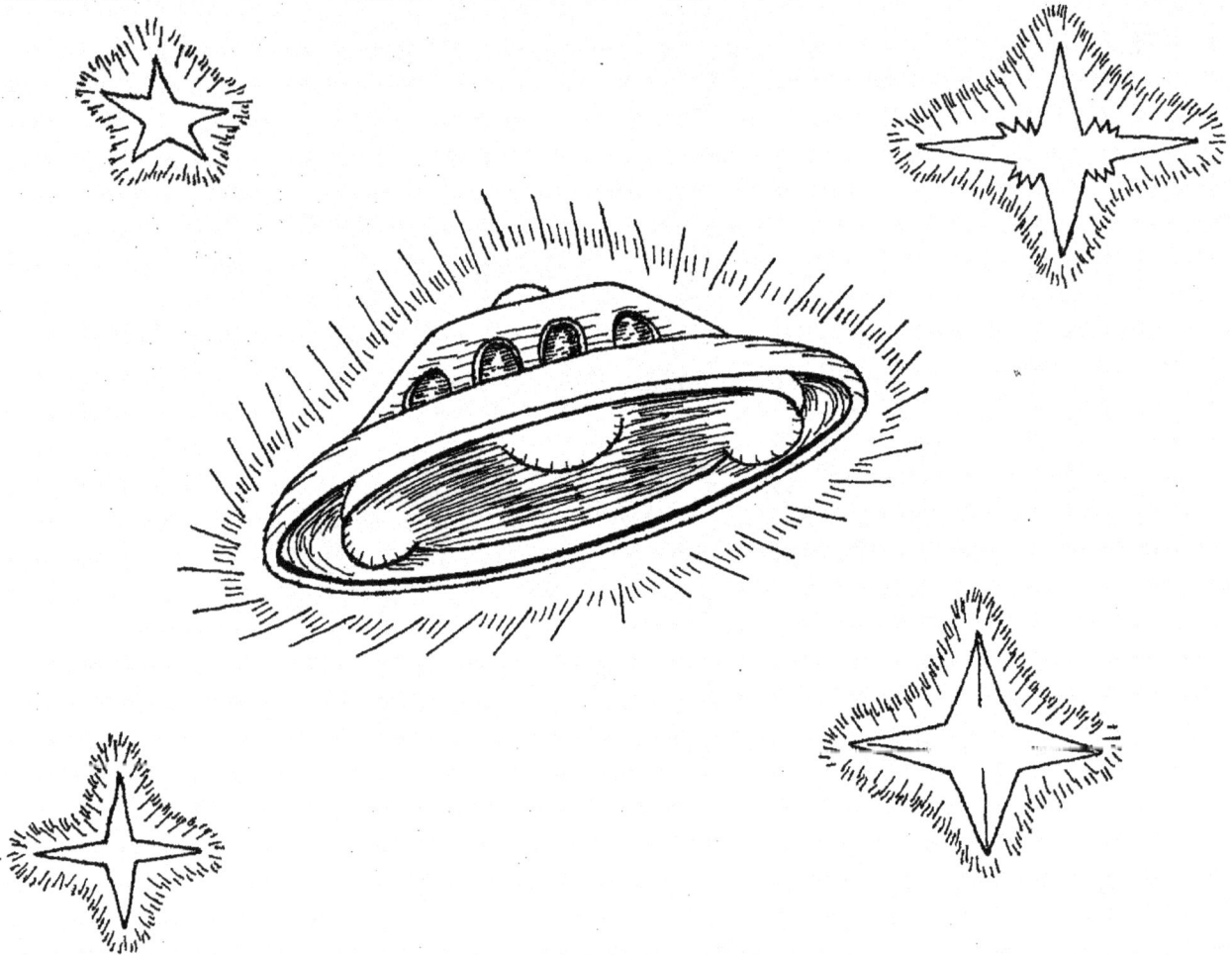

(48)

CHAPTER SEVEN

MISSION ON EARTH: TO LIGHTEN THIS PLANET WITH LOVE

The plan was laid out for me when I was home on Venus, and then instantly erased when I arrived on Earth. As far as I knew, I had to lighten the planet with love as an Earthling. Had I known I would be revealing my true identity, I never could have immersed myself in the role I was assigned to play here.

If one keeps in his or her mind that "it's only a movie" - he or she cannot become totally involved in the plot.

I pursued this girl's dream. It was mine now. I tried to survive while I tried to sing for my survival. But it was deep in me now that I wanted with all my heart to sing for everybody on the Earth, that I could awake them to their feelings.

In the first six years and months I was on Earth, I believed that this was all there was to my mission. The more I tried, the more I failed. The more I cared, the more indifference was shown me. I found out what a lie was and what deception is. And I began hurting inside just as the girl before me.

My determination to sing for the world, turned into desperation. My struggles to stay afloat and keep a shelter, angered my soul, for this struggle to survive on Earth, was intruding on my mission.

I met some of the girl's immediate family, individually, at separate times. They sought me out, and they did not believe I was not her. I was relieved.

I learned how to be funny as the girl before me as a slight covering to shield my feelings. I stayed a loner, worked hard on my craft and awoke each morning with the taste of the song.

I experienced one feeling of Earth-in-love. It was one-sided and awful and unreal. It was simply deep gratitude I felt for this soul on Earth who welcomed my song and allowed me expression of self. But the pain of rejection was increasing. And I was finding it harder and harder to speak at all, at least not anything of what I deeply felt, deeply yet always at the surface of me.

I learned the value of friendship on Earth for it was so rare to find. "Friends" jealous of any slight success I had, "friends" who turned me away when I was in need.

I learned to fear, I learned to mistrust, I learned how to sink into the deepest depressions and soar to the highest highs. I learned to accept joy only when something "good" would come to me.

(49)

Vivenus: Starchild

I became a silent, armless fighter without fighting. I had arms that only wanted to embrace but I had fears now, they would be broken.

I learned discouragement and disappointment. I experienced sickness and defeat. I learned how to feel so tired of it all. I renamed my mission: dream, and I did not let defeat upon defeat keep me down. I refused to play the games most must play on Earth in order to prosper and I was determined in my belief, that the Earth world really wanted honesty, sincerity and "square".

I listened to the "news" outside me, I believed it. And the "bad" theat I heard was happening, made me so sad and this caused me to be even more driven to accomplishing my mission, my dream.

I felt that those in charge were controlling all our lives. That those few who push the buttons, telling us what to think about were in fact, creating for us the lives they wanted us to live.

I wondered about "God" and why He wasn't there to help me. And I wondered why He wasn't there for anybody on Earth who really wanted Him. Good fortune seemed to come to those who took it or who did it on their own.

I began to believe in "luck" and "unluck" and I considered myself in the latter class. I decided that if God was going to continue to ignore my cries to Him for help, that I would thus shut Him out completely and do what I had to do on my own.

I sank deeper and deeper into the quicksand. Until, like the girl before me, I wanted quick passage home. I had tried every Earth way my soul could tolerate, to accomplish my mission. There was just no way left to me. I contemplated suicide but realized that I would not go directly home if I, by my own hand, put an end to my Earth existence.

RELEARNING WORDS OF LOVE

And then (1967) I thought of home and it was the first time since I had been on Earth that I was allowed to re-enter the memories.

Venus Home Star. I could not believe where I was and I could not understand why I had been abandoned here. And mostly, I could not fathom why I had volunteered to come to this planet of sorrow.

I asked for a way to bring God down to help me but I wasn't even sure who I was asking.

My mind was filled with fear about tomorrows and doubts about anything that was good. But somehow I don't know why, I still believed in me. And somehow, I don't know why, I still believed in the love in people even on Earth and even though for the most part, it was not shown to me.

(50)

Vivenus: Starchild

I paralleled the two worlds on which I had lived and was living. They were so different and I wanted to know why. What did the Earth have that Venus did not, that made the Earth people so uncaring of each other? Or what did Venus have that the Earth did not, to make Venus a world of Love?

Venusians live by feelings; Earthlings live by thoughts. Venus, a land of silence; Earth, a planet of noise. Words. It was the only tangible clue I had, that I might be able to do something about. I knew it was my own mind that was stopping my heart from expressing. Perhaps the world of Earth did "get to me" but now, my life was ruled by not the world but what was in my own head.

I realized then that these thoughts in my head I allowed to enter. I believed what I heard, whether it was true or not and if it concerned me in some way, I made it true by believing it.

Then because my background is silence, I realized that thoughts on Earth are no more than a bunch of W-O-R-D-S. And words are only words and yet on Earth, making and breaking lives.

So I decided to put words of love in my mind and erase the words of darkness. I was not sure if I could do it or that if I did it, my mind would set my heart free.

Fear is memorized. So is doubt. It is read to us, said to us, and we repeat it back and repeat it and repeat it until it becomes embedded in our minds. And what is in the mind is brought into existence. An illusion, perhaps, but one that seems to us, so real.

What would love want for me on this planet? What would love want for anyone on this planet or any planet? The best.

I began again and erased the words in my mind. I uprooted the weeds by planting flowers right on top of them. I wrote it down. I spoke it. I taped it. I listened. Words that love would say about every concern within my mind. I isolated myself from my work and acquaintances. I moved from my apartment and the idea that I "had" to have one. I was only concerned with the now. I moved for a one week stay, in a rooming house for women on the other side of New York City. Somehow, I was able to stay there three weeks, and was able to undo the damage that I allowed the Earth to do to my mind.

SHARING MY TRUE IDENTITY AND TRUE SELF

My mind at last agreed with my heart. My mind was clear and I saw the divine pictures as though on a movie reel of the next phase of my mission on Earth. And I was told then by the voice of love, that I was free now to follow my feelings and be guided only by them and that if my mind tried to interrupt it, to remind my mind of the truth.

And then (June-1967) I was given to reveal my true identity and

(51)

share my discovery with the children of Earth. From 1967 to 1972, I was doing just this, being "somebody", speaking to large crowds here and there around the nation.

In this time, I also sat in parks, inviting any, to share in the truth. I was bold about my heritage and so enthusiastic about the simple truth to set the children of Earth free.

I, all through my mission was still being educated in love and through experiences in my life and role, learning how to become one with love, even on Earth.

The limelight is not the true light. And the message was being ignored though I wasn't. Being somebody. By writing this book, if it is love's plan, to be published, will invite aspects of the Earth that is not comforting to my soul. And yet, if in my presence, with my presence, somehow love can comfort you, O' Earth. I am willing to stand if I must, in the limelight again.

I have written several books. I print a few (by love), hand out a few (by love), then put them away in one of the suitcases I carry.

I had a time for just writing and a time for just working in the world as I worked in the silence and learned how to be where I wasn't.

I, for a time, held weekly meetings (which I called "heart-to-hearts"). In them, I sang some of my God-inspired songs and spoke, as love spoke through me.

I learned how to follow feelings. And learned that they are the link to love's plan for me. My feelings, the plan for your feelings, the plan for you. My mind still had thoughts and I still lived in the world but I learned to push the wrong thoughts away, make them take a back seat to love and its statements of beauty and truth.

I became aware of another dimension on Earth. The dimension of darkness, actual souls you cannot see, making me think that what is not me, is me. I learned to discern. I learned to choose who I wanted to represent. Did it represent the light of God, to stay depressed? Did it represent the light of God to complain or critisize or judge another's motives? When you want the prowler to leave your house, the best way is to turn on the light.

All of this and more I learned (and perhaps am still learning) (or at least I still have my "tests" and trials where I must apply the truth of love) while in the service of our Lord, Almighty God, and all of this I learn, not first by His telling me, but by the experience I need to be released from discovering the answer within me.

Once your mind is rid of the Earth debris, once your mind is the light, the doors that were marked "mystery" are opened to you.

(52)

Vivenus: Starchild

Who you are. Where you have been. Why you are here. Where you will go. Why this and that "happens". All is revealed in the light.

Since 1974 I have been walking, ten miles a day, every day, where spirits leads, anywhere USA. Five years of the now eight, I also hitch-hiked to get to where I was to walk for God. And I was and am led to, or waited for those, love had chosen for its say through me. What I say to you, is not what I shall say to her and it is not up to you, is not what I shall say to her and it is not up to me, what is said but up to love. But remember, what step ye stand, I have stood there.

I taught myself (yet by love) how to play the guitar in 1970, at least well enough to accompany myself when I would sing. And since then, I have been writing the songs of my heart and the songs of my experiences, the songs of light and home and the songs of God. For years, I faithfully prepared the songs for the concert for I still have a promise to keep.

Since 1981, I have been putting forth a twelve-page journal called "Feelings, The Venusian Way". I do not advertise, but find my "subscribers" on my walks for God.

My mission on Earth: I used to believe that anything I would do would reach your whole world, but now it seems I believe that what I do, and share is only for a few.

Mine is a solitary life. As I walk for God, I am nameless and unknown. As I speak love, I speak not for myself. I live in silence, but for this. And it's almost heaven on Earth, but I do still seem to have to "survive" one day at a time. Yet, I have learned not to let the Earth's cruelty be my crime. I have learned not to despair when I seem homeless and without, for God who is love, always comes to the rescue and always gets me where He wants me to be.

The tomorrow of my mission, I am not at liberty to reveal here.

The tomorrow of the Earth, I can share.

(53)

CHAPTER EIGHT

THE ROLES I MUST TAKE

One by one find thou thy way, O'child of light, to home. Be on the Earth while ye must be here but be here that you may serve the greater love.

Wait ye for the world's permission and ye shall wait forever.

Two paths have ye to choose from: high path of thy soul and spirit; low path of the flesh. And upon either path, thy Father God will deliver thee instance and circumstance and other souls through which ye will grow closer to the light.

The high path is more glorious to travel and more sweet to thy soul. It will bring a speedier victory to thy role with more understanding and dimension and feeling of purpose. The path of light is the direct path to home. It is a path of love, of truth, of dignity. And it is a path assured; you may walk in confidence.

Awake ye children of Earth, and choose now thy path. Ye have not "forever" to decide. This is the time to step over the fence ye straddle, knowing and believing in the light, yet not always acting in it.

For thy "friends" may laugh and ye might lose them. Thy "family" might scold, and they might disown thee. Who are thy friends but friends in the light? Who is the family but those who love love?

The world of Earth as it appears now, is the play-field of the darkness. Fear and doubt and indifference, despair, depression, lifelessness. This is not love's plan. Why are ye in it? Can you not get out?

It is for this I have come, to awake you to your feelings, not by my words but by my life.

And so I have stood hours and hours in feet of snow, bag and baggage in the role of "hitch-hiker all in white" and the Earth people drove by in their cars and trucks. Some expressed horror, some amusement, some concern, some even anger. It was only a feeling for a moment as they whizzed by but they felt. And some who were moved, took the next step and acted on their feelings and realized they could alleviate their pain for me by stopping and offering me a ride.

Rain and snow and heat and sun, winds to terrify. I understood that you might feel and recognize that you were feeling. And I waited to see if you would act on it.

And I walked and I walked and I am still walking, having nothing but the spirit to lead me to you. I turn in a door, I tell you I walk for God. I seem to be in need and you lie to me or you laugh at

(54)

me or you are concerned for me or you feel above me and I wait to
see you act what you are feeling.

There is only one who gives, that one is God, living in each of
you, waiting to express and come alive. It feels so much better to
give than to receive. Yet, I have played the role of what seemed like
a "beggar"; that God could live on planet Earth.

KNOWING THE TRUTH AND NOT BEING AFRAID OF IT

I do not feel that there could be a greater service to love,
to God, that I could render.

Those in the seeming position of "power" on Earth, have intimid-
ated you, and your feelings of concern for a brother or sister (stranger
or not) on your planet, stay concealed.

Feelings, that O' Earth children of light, is what you must re-
trieve from the heartless hands of ignorance. Those that lead you,
shall fall into their own pits, and shall continue to try to pull you
down with them.

How long will you allow it? How long will you stand silently in
the wings, watching them, listening to them flub their lines yet
continuing to let their foolish drama go on?

The plan of love is the only plan for all the worlds including the
planet Earth. It matters not what seems and appearances are deceiving.

By your faith, you bring it to pass. What is your faith in?

When I first stepped onto the Earth ground in 1960, this planet
of Earth was saturated in fear. Fear; faith that the worst will come.
And now twenty-one years later (1982), this planet of Earth is saturated
in depression. Depression: faith that the worst has come. The plan
is love. What do you know of love? What do you feel when you love?
What is your prayer and wish and hope for who and what you love?

Is it not the very best that can be? Will you not do anything in
your power to help the one you love? Will you not do anything in
your power to bring happiness to who you love?

That is love's plan for all its children. And it is not something
you have to wait for. And it is not something that will "just happen"
to you and to the Earth. It is something you must claim.

Bypass the truth, and your soul is restless. Resist love's ways
and your path seems to lead you nowhere.

Nothing and no one on the outside of you, will bring you "happiness"
for more than a moment. Return to love and feel contentment that will
not leave you. Return to your feelings and start back to the joy of
life.

(55)

Vivenus: Starchild

Not all of what you feel is joyful, but that you will feel it through, will bring you the reward.

Be not afraid to remember. Pray for light and trust light to take you on the incredible journey of your soul.

Are you fearful to be free in spirt? Are you fond of material comforts and fixed in your mind that you must fit in with the world of Earth? Are you ashamed to admit you love God and want more than anything to feel His love for you?

Do you not know you have a choice what comes into your mind? And ye have a choice what you will allow to stay there. Do you not know you do not have to listen to liars and do not have to be robbed by the thieves of the night?

Do you not know by now, that what you believe in your heart is the truth? If it were not, it would have left you by now. The thoughts in your mind change. Your philosophies and opinions stem from your experiences. Your heart never changes its mind. Do you not know by now, you can trust it?

Within your heart, lives God who keepeth every promise.

Change your words, children of light, that only love is spoken. Remove thyself from "making conversation". Turn off the news programs, tune in to the universe of love.

THE BELIEF OF GOD THRU LOVE

The power that is in God, is in you. He spoke the word and it happened and it was. And the same law and power is within you. Speak the word you want to be and it is done. The power of the word governs the Earth: then let us make the word be true and holy.

"...Let there be light...", "and there was light."

Ye are not sheep, Earth, ye are only parrots repeating the words repeated to you. And the words became manifest.

Change the images in your mind to perfection to how you want things and people to be. Clean your house; take out the garbage and you will feel at home again.

If you want the snows of winter to be gone, stare not out the window in despair but close thy eyes and picture the spring flowers, the green grass and tree with leaves. And when more than half the minds on Earth or even in one area, pictures the spring as it will be as though it is now, the winter will cease and the spring will appear.

One by one, this world of Earth will be lifted into light. And when more than half the minds are concentrated on love's divine pictures

(56)

then the planet will be restored to light.

Love's law works both ways as you O'Earth, can see. For more than half the minds on Earth right now much more are focused on the appearance and the mirage and not on the reality of love.

There is nothing to get "sick" about unless your soul does not like what you are doing or where you are going or unless your soul has chosen the experience.

Pray for what love wants and love will have the victory in you.

Pray for your mind to believe what your heart already knows. Pray for the strength to work at it. Pray to keep the darkness from you. Follow your feelings and follow your destiny.

Call on love, greatest power in all the universe is in you. Be still and know God.

Prayer: the quickest way to the mountain's top. Prayer is heard, is always answered. Believe ye receive. Prepare to receive. Trust love's timing.

Can you see a thought? Can you see a feeling? Yet, these invisibles are what make you, you, and him, him, and her, her. All that is created, is simply brought down. All that is visible, began an invisible. Trust love is working on your behalf, even when you cannot yet see the results. Tune in to what you feel and be reassured that love, who makes the sun to rise and the sun to set on planet Earth, knows the perfect time for all things under it.

Your conscious mind commands your ship. Your subconscious mind is your private servant, bringing to you what your conscious mind dictated. Your superconscious mind is God which you will hear and feel when the commander of your ship aims for the sea of beauty.

What is on Venus, shall be on Earth. It is the plan, love plan.

THE GUIDING LIGHT

When the hearts and minds on Earth are one in agreement within each being then shall there be peace on Earth. It is a one by one process. And not until the last runner has crossed the finish line is the marathon concluded.

How long shall this take? We do not know. But we do know that the planet Earth cannot survive much longer with darkness upon it. There is a time and a season for every world to run its tether. And then, the Father must save His world and lift it into light. Those who are with the light shall be lifted with the light and those who still choose to remain in the darkness shall be reborn on a new world where light and darkness may live and learn together and through each other.

(57)

Vivenus: Starchild

This time is not far off. It cannot be. We have seen the signs. Love will not destroy what it created. Life could never create "death."

When the petals fall from the Earth flower, when the flower's center seems to wither and "die", do you really believe that is the end of that flower? Does it not return to you in the very same spot, the very next spring? Love reminds you, O' Earth, of eternal life.

O' learn of light, Earth, and your love will not be so fragile. Learn of light and your love will not stop and start and stop and start but flow into forever.

Call on the light. It is your armour and your shield. Let love's angels unseen shine the light on something or someone you cannot find. Call on light to turn your wheel from the path of danger. Call on the light when you don't like what you feel. Call on the light when you don't understand with your heart.

Remember love's laws, love's ways is a circle. Love waits for you; you do not wait for it.

I could write down everything I know and it would still be nothing. For the truth is that the truth is within you and it is no less than the truth that is within me.

I am really not here to "teach" but to love. And my mission on Earth is not yet completed.

And so I walk, I talk, I write, I sing, I pray and I dream of doing something magnificent for God.

How shall I repay Him, for all His benefits to me?

And so, from Venus Home Star I journeyed in space to Earth on a mission: to lighten this planet with love.

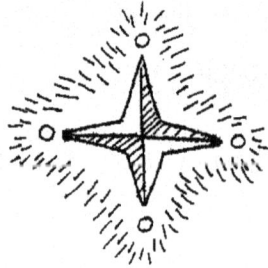

(58)

A PORTFOLIO

MISSION on EARTH

VIVENUS
MAILING ADDRESS
PO BOX 5
GALILEE
PENNSYLVANIA 18423

(59)

WALKING FOR GOD

OREGON -- PORTLAND 1974
GRESHAM-MILWAUKIE 1979
SANDY-TROUTDALE
CLACKAMAS-LAKE OSWEGO 1979
ESTACADA-GLADSTONE
OREGON CITY-BEAVERTON
SALEM-ROSEBURG
GRANTS PASS-CAVE JUNCTION

CRESCENT CITY 1978
A EUREKA-UKIAH
L WILLITS-UKIAH
I SAN RAFAEL
F SAN FRANCISCO 1975
O OAKLAND-SAN MATEO-NEWARK
R FREMONT-MILPITAS-PALO ALTO 1978
N MENLO PARK-SUNNYVALE
I MT. VIEW-SAN JOSE 1979
A SANTA CLARA--CAMPBELL 1981
CUPERTINO-SARATOGA 1980
LOS GATOS-GILROY
LOS ALTOS HILLS 1979
HOLLISTER-SALINAS
MONTEREY-MARINA
PASO ROBLES, PISMO BEACH

1981 OAK VIEW / BAT CORRY PARK
SANTA PAULA / NEWBURG
CAMARILLO / CAMPARIME
MORE MUGRENE / PORT HUENEME
FILLMORE 1976 / SANTA 1977
PARADISE POINT 1977 / DANA BEACH
SOLANA / DEL MAR
LA JOLLA / LA MESA

MORRO BAY, OBISPO
SAN LUIS OBISPO 1979
COSTA MESA-SANTA MARIA 1980
SAN CLEMENTE-VISTA-WESTWOOD
SAN JUAN CAPISTRANO-LAGUNA BEACH
SANTA GRANDE TORRANCE 1976
SHELL BEACH-OCEANO
SAN LUIS 1976
SAN DIEGO-CARLSBAD 1981
NEWPORT BEACH-CARLSBAD 1981
OCEANSIDE-SAN CLEMENTE 1981
EL CAJON--EL CENTRO 1975
ALPINE--SAN DIEGO
SANTA MONICA-REDONDO BEACH 1976
SAN BERNARDINO-SAN MARCOS
1,000 OAKS--SAN BERNARDINO-SANTWOOD
ARROYO GRANDE-GOLETA 1981
ARROYO BARBARA-VENTURA
CARPINTERIA-VENTURA 1976
LOS ANGELES 1977

MONTANA
BILLINGS-BOZEMAN 1975

SOUTH DAKOTA 1975
SIOUX FALLS

NEVADA 1976
LAS VEGAS 1976

WYOMING 1975
LARAMIE
SHERIDAN

UTAH 1976
GREEN RIVER
SALINA

COLORADO 1976
BYERS
DENVER
GRAND JUNCTION

MINNESOTA
ALBERT LEA 1975

WISCONSIN
MADISON

MICHIGAN 1975
WOODS--HARPER WOODS PRAIRIE B.F. WOODS
DETROIT-DETROIT FARMS--FERNDALE
EAST POINTE
GROSSE OAK
ROYAL BIRMINGHAM

ILLINOIS 1975
CHICAGO
ROCKFORD
SPRINGFIELD 1977
BLOOMINGTON 1976 **INDIANA**
INDIANAPOLIS

MISSOURI
SPRINGFIELD
ST. LOUIS

OHIO - DAYTON
ONDALIA-TIPP CITY-SIDNEY
VANDALIA-PIQUA
TROY-ROSEVILLE-KETTERING
SKYDINE-FARGO
READING-LENFS
NEW CARLISLE-COLUMBUS
NEWBERRY-DAYTON
HUBERTING

KENTUCKY 1977--1981
LOUISVILLE
BOWLING GREEN
BONDVILLE
ELIZABETHTON
CARROLLTON

TENNESSEE
KNOXVILLE
MEMPHIS 1977
NASHVILLE 1981

MISSISSIPPI
VICKSBURG-CLINTON
EDWARDS-SARDIS
GRENADA-MERANDO 1981
COMO-MEMPHIS

LOUISIANA 1974
JENNINGS
JETTER CITY
BOSSI MONROE 1981

TEXAS
EL PASO 1977
VAN HORN
DECOHANS
BIG SPRING
COAHOMA
ST. STOCKTON
KAT STOCKTON
ST. ROCKSIDE
SULLEROE
SULLERFORD
ABSTELLFORD
BASTLEKFORD
ELLER-VIEW
LONGVIEW 1981
MARSHALL

NEW MEXICO 1975--1981
GALLUP
LAS CRUCES 1976
DEMING
LORDSBURG

ARIZONA 1977
TUCSON
TUMA-MESA
PHOENIX-MESA 1975
TEMPE-GLENDALE
PRESCOTT-GRANDE-WILCOX 1976
TEXAS GRANDE
CASA GERO
GILA BEND 1981
GLOBE

OKLAHOMA
SAYRE CITY 1981
ELK CITY

ARKANSAS
RUSSELLVILLE 1981
MORRILTON
LENANKE

GEORGIA
MACON-TIFTON
VALDOSTA
DALTON

PENNSYLVANIA 1981
HARRISBURG
WASHINGTON
BENTLE VERNON
BELLE VERNON
GREENSBURG
BOSWELL
EVERETTSBURG
CHARLESTOWN
PARK-LEHEM
BETHLEHEM
CUMBERLAND
STROUDSBURG
SCRANTON CITY
CARDREST
CORRYFIELD
JERSEY FIELD

NEW YORK 1981
NARROWSBURG
LIBERTY
JEFFERVIS
PORT JEK
MONTICELLO
HALIFAX MANOR
LIVINGSTON
LEWISVILLE
EDGSTER
ONEOTTA
MIDDLETOWN
HURTZBORO
OSWEGO-ARKVILLE

MARYLAND
WILLIAMSPORT
HANCOCK

WEST VIRGINIA
FAIRMONT
CLARKSBURG
SALEM
PARKERSBURG

FLIVE OAK 1977
L JACKSONVILLE
O JASPER
R LAKE CITY
I ALACHUA
D HIGH SPRINGS
A NEWBERRY
WILLISTON
MACLENNY
ELLISVILLE
GAINESVILLE
OCALA BEACH
DUNEDIN BEACH
CLEARWATER

TOTALS AS OF _November 81_
CITIES: 296
GOD-MILES WALKED: 17,756
VIV-SONGS WRITTEN: 81

FEELINGS -- THE VENUSIAN WAY -- 12 PAGE JOURNAL WRITTEN BY VIV EVERY OTHER MONTH PUBLISHED BY LOVE

COPYRIGHT 1981 VIVENUS FULL YEAR SUBSCRIPTION AT LOVE OFFERING

VIVENUS PO BOX 5 GALILEE PA 18423

Ⓞakland Ⓣribune SUNDAY

Gannett Newspaper   July 13, 1980/Oakland, California

★★ ★★ A-17

Campaign '80

A Venusian visitor goes campaigning

By Susan Shoemaker
Tribune Staff Writer

It was late last year, while VIVenus was contemplating the generally sorry state of the nation, that the idea first came to her: God for President.

It took a few months for the notion to take hold, but by spring she was convinced it was the right thing to do. Now Viv is on the stump, managing a campaign for God as a write-in candidate in the November election.

The theme of the campaign is "It's Not Odd to Vote for God."

Viv — who claims to be a Venusian who came to Earth in 1967 and moved into the body of a woman from New York — is spreading the word through brochures, buttons, matchbooks and a dirge-like theme song that she wrote herself. She has sent tapes of the mournful tune, accompanied by a brief plug for her candidate, to newspapers and television and radio stations across the country.

"It's God for President!" she harmonizes in a strong, deep voice. "So go become a resident! Write him in and we can win! And come election day we'll say, 'Oh, it's not odd to vote for God ... ' "

God has no platform and no party, and according to Viv, doesn't particularly enjoy campaigning.

"He doesn't want to run, but he wants to win," she said from campaign headquarters in a Morgan Hill motel.

And if he does win, "there would be sharing and no fear — that's the main thing. It would be like heaven and like home."

In order to be counted as a write-in in California, would-be candidates must file statements with the secretary of state's

Tribune photo by Leo Cohen

VIVenus outside headquarters of her one ... ahh ... person campaign.

office containing a signature and a home address, among other things.

Viv acknowledged that getting the form filled out could be a problem.

"I think I might just leave it on my desk and see if it magically gets signed," she said.

But spokesmen for the secretary of state say they would reject any such filing because state law requires that candidates for office be "persons."

And beyond that, they suggest that God might not meet U.S. constitutional

requirements that the president be at least 35 years old (no problem there), a natural-born citizen of the United States (uncertain) and a resident of the country for at least 14 years (sometimes seems most unlikely).

"Anyway," said one staffer in Sacramento, "the last we heard, she was living in Brazil."

Viv, however, is not concerned about such mundane obstacles.

"I don't feel any real anxiety about it," she said. "It's all up to God.

"And if he wants it, he'll get it."

- 61 -

Viv of Venus Claims Her Role Is to Bring Love to Earthlings

By ART SPINELLA

The first report of "flying saucers" to receive general acclaim in the United States came in 1946. Before and since that time there were and have been stories of "people from other worlds."

But when one says he or she is from another planet or claims to have met beings from another world there are smirks and scepticism.

Viv of Venus is a petite girl with short, dark hair and eyes from a Walter Keane painting—large, round and expressive.

She says she is from the planet Venus and the initial reaction is to smile knowingly.

* * *

WHETHER OR not she actually is from Venus is academic. It may well be a "publicity stunt," but no matter where she is "from" Viv of Venus has a philosophy.

Her mission here on Earth is "to enlighten this planet with love."

"My main goal, the reason I have been placed here on Earth by the Divine Being, is to bring love to the people of Earth," she explains.

Without the slightest trace of Midwest "twang," Southern drawl or New York accent detectable to a nonexpert, one is apt to speculate that Viv either has taken a great number of speech courses or has been able to learn "broadcasting" speech to a very fine degree.

VIV OF VENUS

"I CAME TO Earth in 1960 and took the place of a girl who committed suicide. This girl had many dreams for the world and I attempted to work toward those dreams in a normal earthly fashion," Viv explained. "Three years ago I discovered that I, too, was beginning to believe those words which make Earth people hate each other. Words such as doubt, fear and wrong.

"I decided then that if I could not accomplish my mission through Earthly ways I would try an unearthly way."

Viv explained that love is the only way to open people's minds and take the negative forces from the world.

* * *

"IT IS NECESSARY for a person to tune out the negative forces in this world and tune in with the one overall Mind and stay in tune without depending on anyone or anything outside of the individual."

According to Viv, institutions such as government and marriage are "confining" but do not hurt.

"I am not here to knock down or destroy anything," she said. "I am here to guide people to a better way of life. Institutions are not wrong, they do not damage a society, but they do confine the freedom a person should have and deserves. These institutions will fall by the side as people become more and more understanding."

* * *

VIV DOES NOT speak much of the planet Venus.

"People begin asking what type of furniture we have and what we eat. All I can say that would be of any use to people on Earth is that we do not have government, we do not have fear and we do not have wars. People there have learned to move according to their own feelings. They are not inhibited."

People on Earth have to learn to trust their own judgment, claims Viv.

(See VIV, 10-A)

Viv
(Continued from 3-A)

"There is no reason to always be serious. There is no reason not to accept people as they are rather than prejudging them. When a person expects bad in another person he will find it."

* * *

VIV OF VENUS is scheduled to speak at the Unity Center of Birmingham, 1152 Bennaville, Sunday at 8 p.m. The minister of the Center, Ernest Ramsey, commented on why Viv is speaking there.

"She is a genuine and sincere person who appeals to the younger people. Her ideas are in harmony with ours," said Ramsey.

The meeting will be open to the public and there is no predetermined time for the end of the meeting.

BEFORE COMING to Michigan, Viv spent a great deal of time in Portland, Ore.; San Francisco, Calif. and New York.

"For nearly four months I spent every day in Central Park in the same spot, hanging four handmade sings on the hedges and allowing only love and God to work through me. Every day was like a miracle. People changed before my eyes. Violence dissolved into kindness, hurt into laughter. Fear and confusion washed away to be replaced by love," she said.

From Venus? An instrument of the Lord? Believers and skeptics alike would have to admit that if nothing else, Viv is an

Girl From Venus Tells Of Coming

By PETER C. WOLF, JR.
Staff Writer

Imagine, you are a new reporter for a newspaper and given the normal run-of-the-mill (not too great) stuff to cover.

Then it happens, your boss goes on vacation and you have to take his place for two weeks. You wonder what you are going to do for front page news.

Somebody tells you there is a girl, who says she is from Venus, living on your beat. You panic. That might be worth front page, after all how many stories do you read about real live Venusians living here on earth.

You get up tight and decide to interview her. You phone and a man answers: "Miss Venus is taking no calls but you can have an interview at 3 p.m."

Being a cub reporter trying to make good, you decide to play it straight.

She meets you at the door, looking a little Venusian you think, yet mostly earthling. You are asked in, and to look like a real professional get out your light meter and test the room for photography.

Miss Venus, acting extremely cool, sits waiting to start the interview. You panic.

You open with, "Tell me what life is like on Venus."

She says "Physically similar, but mentally superior and much more wonderful."

"Is there weather?"

"No."

"Is the form or body you are in the same as on Venus?"

"No, earth-form is heavier and thicker."

By now you know you aren't going to shake her on anything. You take a few pictures and let her talk.

She asks about your paper: "Is it daily?"

"No, weekly."

"What is it made up of?"

"Good news, no accidents or murders just the happier stuff that the dailies can't fit in."

"That sounds wonderful, I wouldn't feel like I am on earth anymore if there is such a paper."

"The worst thing we have to print is the obituary," I say. She says that is not bad since all those who die go to a better life.

You drop the interview idea altogether and play it straight in an attempt to retreat but you realize you have let yourself go.

You let her interview you.

Actually, "Viv" Venus is an alien being from the sun's second-closest planet. She has come to earth in a flying saucer and taken the identity of a girl who secretly committed suicide. She did not originally plan to expose herself. It just happened.

Her mission is to get people to believe in the younger generation's "love not war" philosophy. A noble cause. But I doubt if even a Venusian could bridge the generation gap.

At least, the main idea comes across. People who expect the worst will get the worst.

Miss Venus, currently staying at 3620 SE 84th Ave., will leave the Portland area shortly and head for Detroit. She says there are many different planetary representatives on earth. She also says there is life on all the planets.

It seems that in America's Apollo 11 experience, everybody on the moon must have been on vacation. Anyway who cares? According to Venus, everything is going to groove within 20 years.

VIV VENUS is her name and the last name is also name of her planet. She is on earth presenting the Venus view that we should make 'love not war' here on earth. While in Portland she is staying at 3620 SE 84th Ave.

VENUS may be second closest to the Sun but it has a representative here on Earth. Viv Venus is currently visiting Portland giving talks to residents concerning the better world Earth will be in 1990.

(63)

Vivenus: Starchild

SCRANTON TIMES - SCRANTON, PA.

Woman Walks 30,000 Miles for God

By JOE VINANSKY
Upvalley Bureau

Carbondale — "Belief consists in accepting the affirmations of the soul; unbelief, in denying them.",

Ralph Waldo Emerson may have penned these words but Viv Enus has lived them.

Driven by a personal conviction, she has spent the past eight years traveling throughout the United States "walking for God." During that time, she has logged nearly 30,000 miles and written over 80 songs about her experiences.

As Ms. Enus explained, since Christmas 1974, she has walked 10 miles a day "living day-by-day and going where the Lord takes me carrying his message."

"I walk because I need to share God with others . . . to tell of his love that so few people are aware of," said Ms. Enus.

The Times spoke with Ms. Enus while she was traveling through Carbondale. At first, she was somewhat hesitant to discuss her life upon discovering that she was dealing with a reporter, but later agreed to talk about her philosophy as well as her controversial past.

According to Ms. Enus, she began her long trek to express feelings that others weren't willing to express.

"When I write a song, that song is your song. I'm only expressing what other people are afraid to say," explained Ms. Enus. "When I speak with people, I talk about the love of God. That's all there is. If people would realize this if they'd stop worrying, . . . trying to please everyone else, the world wouldn't suffer from all its problems."

Not only has Ms. Enus written a number of songs, but she also authored five books which "are still on hold" with her publisher until she "gets around to seeing him."

However, her most challenging endeavor to date has been a "Draft God for President Campaign" that she initiated in 1980. "I started the idea that it's not odd to vote for God for president, but it wasn't started early enough," said Ms. Enus. "It really wasn't a joke. It could have gotten big enough to get God on the mind of our nation on on election day. Maybe people

would have started to pray to God for help."

Although she gained notoriety from her presidential campaign, it doesn't compare with the notoriety she received from 1967 through 1972 because of her willingness to share "the truth she had discovered."

Even though she tends to downplay her past, she did admit that she received "a lot of publicity because of a claim she had made."

"I became a somebody because of what I claimed about myself and where I was from," said Ms. Enus. "During this time period, I spoke at places about these truths that I had found. But people were more interested in me and my claim than what I was sharing. People were more interested in me and I didn't like that. I wasn't living the truth anymore."

When questioned about her claim, she said, "I firmly believe that my soul is from the planet Venus. This is a long story which I'm tired of telling because of the way it's been blown out of proportion."

She added that "most peo-

ple who have any faith worry about where they're going to go after the Earth. If they think they're going someplace afterward, they must have been someplace before," explained Ms. Enus. "I just know that we were someplace before we came to Earth. Why would God create such a vast universe and only have life on one planet — Earth?" asked Ms. Enus.

Like others who have made similar claims, Ms. Enus has received her share of public abuse and scorn because of her beliefs. "Sure, people will be skeptical while others have ridiculed me. It used to bother me but not now. It's difficult speaking because you're very vulnerable. But I don't worry about it because God protects me."

Currently she publishes a journal entitled "Feelings — The Venusian Way," which she describes as "Something new, something honest, something bold, something daring, something free, something you, something true, something deep, something warm, something not afraid to say this is me."

She publishes the journal

every other month but says she doesn't worry about making money from it. Instead, she lives from day to day working at odd jobs to make just enough money to subsidize her traveling and printing costs.

According to Ms. Enus, all of us have to learn to trust love. "There is a plan for everyone. It's a matter of letting yourself be guided by feeling and letting your head step out of the way. After all, love is more powerful than thoughts."

"We could reach that ideal state . . . of peace, no fears . . . a perfect love. It's a matter of putting our faith in God and trusting his plan. Basically, that's the truth I'm trying to share," said Ms. Enus.

Ms. Enus doesn't argue with her critics who describe her as "unusual," "not all there," and some other names that can't be mentioned in a newspaper.

She just smiles and continues walking. After all, she realizes that she isn't the first person who has been criticized for speaking about love.

(64)

Vivenus: Starchild

THE OREGON JOURNAL TUESDAY, AUGUST 5, 1969   2M

'THINK GOOD, FEEL GOOD, BE GOOD'

Viv Venus Visits Portland, Sees Coming Of Worldwide Love

By ROLLA J. CRICK
Journal Staff Writer

By 1980, said the girl who claims to be from Venus, earth will be a planet of love.

People will think good, feel good and be good and will be happy all of the time without aid from a middle man — an entertainer.

War will be passe. The theory of the hippies will be fact: to make love, not war, is man's destiny.

PROCLAIMING the message of love in Portland this week via newspapers, radio and television is a girl who calls herself Viv Venus. In a "heart to heart" talk at 7:30 p.m. Thursday in the Community Room of Western Savings & Loan Association, NE 42d Ave. and Sandy Blvd., she will offer the same message.

She looks, walks and talks like an earth girl, but she says that she came from the planet Venus nine years ago.

She says that she took the place of her physical double, an earth girl who committed suicide in New York state, and for the past three years has been carrying out a mission of lighting earth with love.

THE BILLIONS of dollars and rubles being spent by the governments of the U.S. and USSR to learn whether life exists elsewhere are basically wasted, if you believe Viv Venus.

Here is what she says:

— People who look like earth people populate Venus. They live in houses without roofs or floors and they communicate by telepathy.

— There are no watches or calendars on Venus. ("Time is eternal, so why do you need a thing on your wrist?" she asks.)

— THERE ARE no mirrors on Venus. ("No one worries about looks. Life is a blessing without mirrors.")

— Grass is white and soft on Venus. Trees are in many colors, and there is no money. ("We don't need it.")

— Villages on Venus are created out of the thoughts of people. ("People don't live in theaters like here. There is a village there where the earth world is represented and where words are spoken in

plays.")

VIV VENUS learned some earth words in that village, she says. The rest of her audible vocabulary was learned on her way here on a "swoop," (a flying saucer).

When her earth counterpart committed suicide, she was gathered up on one side of the "swoop" while Viv Venus was "landed" on the other side.

For six years, claims Viv, she lived as the earth girl, not knowing that eventually she was to reveal her true identity. She refuses to disclose the identity of the earthling, saying it is immaterial.

When her mission is done here she will return to Venus. ("How I don't know, nor when, but it doesn't matter," she says.

MOST MINDS on earth, she

continues, are conditioned to here. I drove to Portland from expect the worst, and that is Detroit and all the way I was what they get. "People must impressed with the many do as I did — I brainwashed empty, open spaces," she myself with good. What you says. look for is what you get and if For the next few weeks Viv you look for good you will re- will reside at the home of Mr. ceive it." and Mrs. Zelrun Karsleigh, 3620 SE 84th Ave.

Earth's worry about over-population is one of the planet's many "imaginary untruths," says Viv Venus.

"If people have any trust in love, in God, in the creator or whatever you want to call it, they would know that too many people would not be put

VIV VENUS

Vivenus: Starchild

'It's not odd to vote for God'

'It's not odd to vote for God'

By Jennifer Foote
Staff writer

"Now hear this: God is in the race and running for President of the United States" — ViVenus.

If you jeer at Jimmy, tire of Ted, reject Ronald and agonize over Anderson — don't panic yet about the big blank on your November ballot. The latest candidate to join the race could be The One. As a matter of fact, this contender already has an enthusiastic following.

Yes, God himself has reportedly tossed his hat into the ring, and will run as a write-in candidate, according to his campaign manager ViV, who claims she is a native of the planet Venus. The 20-earth-year-old alien and her supporters will officially kick off the "holy campaign"

with a rally in San Jose, possibly July 4.

"It's not odd to vote for God," is the theme of the effort. Buttons, matchbooks and fliers bearing the slogan are already being distributed, along with a tape recording of ViV singing a song called, you guessed it, "It's Not Odd."

That tape recording, along with a press release, arrived at The Argus office Friday morning.

ViV, who said she has a conversation with her candidate every day regarding the campaign, is confident about the election.

"God can't lose," she said. "Ultimately, he'll be counting the votes anyway".

However, God could be the only one to count those votes.

To qualify as a write-in candidate on the November ballot, God would have to sign a declaration of intent to run and give his home address, according to the Alameda County Registrar of Voters Jim Riggs.

"He wouldn't necessarily have to be a California resident," said Riggs. "But he would have to meet constitutional requirements.

"In other words, God would have to be at least 35 years old, a natural-born citizen of the United States and a 14-year resident of the country".

However, Riggs pointed out that if God were a U.S. citizen before the adoption of the U.S. Constitution, he could still qualify.

Continued back of section, col. 1

'It's not odd to vote for God'

Continued from Page 1

"As far as I know, God didn't run in the primaries or in another election," said Riggs. "But if we get the paperwork, we will count his votes."

In this year's primary, someone called Secrede Lorile-Chrisse Amercanse Dorothye Devile Gode Hillh was a write-in candidate for the Democratic write-in opted for the nomination under the name (or names) Charlie C. Compton a.k.a. Charlie a.k.a. White Horse Charlie a.k.a. The White Horse a.k.a. The White Horse Entry a.k.a. Black Horse a.k.a. The Black Horse Entry a.k.a. Jockey a.k.a. "C" a.k.a. The Horseman a.k.a. Whitellorse-Jockey.

Meanwhile, ViVenus is plugging away from her Morgan Hill campaign headquarters. And what can we expect if God wins the election?

"It's up to him," said ViVenus. "The difference between God and the other candidates," she added reverently, "is that he keeps his promises."

THE ARGUS

Serving Fremont, Newark and Union City, California, Saturday, June 14, 1980

Vol. 18, No. 47   28 Pages   15 cents

Vivenus: Starchild

NAME			PLACE		LONG.	LAT.
VIVENUS			NEW YORK City		74W	41N
MONTH	DATE	YEAR	HOUR	S.t For m.p	asc.	S.R.
Sept	24	1960	10:03 P.m	22:19	3°2' ♊	—

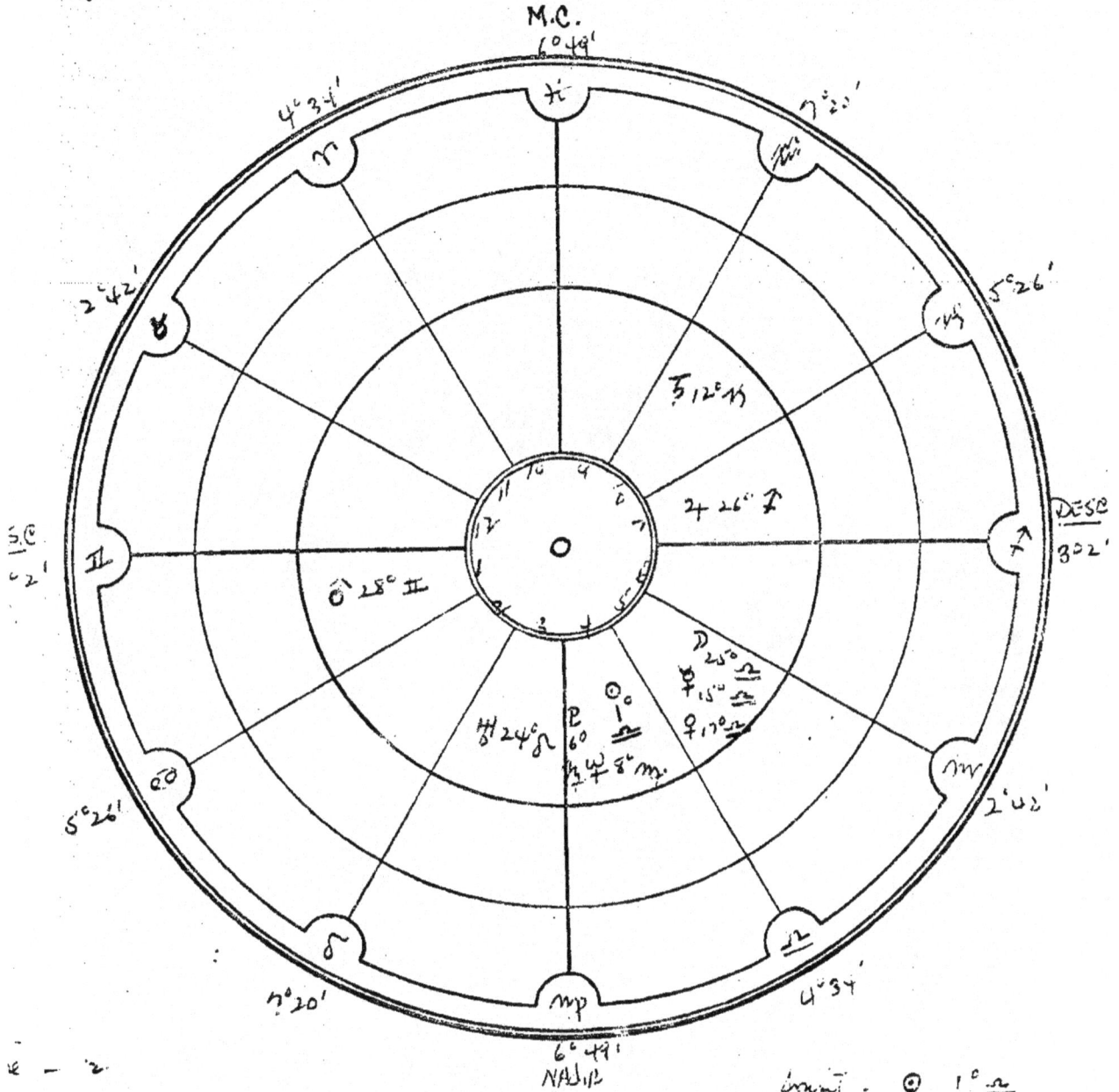

CHART OF THE DAY VIVENUS ARRIVED ON EARTH

Vivenus: Starchild

Flying Saucer Revelations

by

Michael X

Flying Saucer Revelations

Michael X Prophet
Of The Golden Age
Of Flying Saucers

by Timothy Green Beckley

His real name was Michael Barton, though he wrote over 25 tomes under the moniker of simply Michael X. Why? Perhaps to add a bit of intrigue to his wanderings amongst the New Age communities of Southern California. He was well known to followers who would gather at places like Giant Rock in the Mojave Desert to exchange stories of meeting beautiful, benevolent, angelic-like beings from outer space, said to be zipping through the crisp blue California sky in silvery ships known in those "golden days" as Flying Saucers.

All we really know is that Michael was a simple businessman who had a friend whose life was saved from cancer after having a close encounter. A former skeptic, Barton began to question his sensibilities as he spoke with many of the UFO "contactees" who reportedly had entertained human-looking aliens face-to-face, but also maintained they had been inside these cigar and disc-shaped craft and had even gone for trips to other planets.

It was all very wild – almost illusionary – but it was all too real to those who followed the exploits of such well known contactees as George Adamski, George Van Tassell, Truman Bethrum, George Hunt Williamson, and the one and only Dana Howard -- one of the few female members of this select cosmic community whose works we have recently reprinted.

Michael X was one of the better writers of the era. He knew how to turn a word as Long John Nebel would like to say on his all night talk show devoted largely to the stories of the flying saucer contactees. But Michael X didn't just write about lights in the sky --or about close encounters for that matter.

Flying Saucer Revelations

No, Michael X got his information first hand via telepathy from his extraterrestrial "guides." And they taught him much; everything from health secrets to how their understand of science, philosophy and religion, could propel us forward into a New Age of reason.

And above all else – Michael X shared what he learned from the "Venusians" -- who he said were his closest acquaintances – in a series of very concise study guides which he sold mainly at UFO and metaphysical meetings, but also advertised in publications like Fate and Ray Palmer's Flying Saucers From Outer Space magazine. In fact, truth be told, I was selling Michael X's books when I was 15. We would advertise them in our little mimeographed publications and Michael would drop ship them to our readers. He had books on cosmic telepathy, how to initiate contact with the UFOnauts, health secrets, visions at Fatima, Nazi UFO secrets and so forth. Before he vanished from the scene he sold most of his books to Gray Barker of Saucerian Press.

When Barker passed I purchased all the remaining copies and had them lying around in various cubbyholes. We feel that readers today deserve to read what Michael X had to say so the following material is a natural adjunct to the work of Vivenus. We hope you will read it and be overwhelmed and enlightened as we were several decades ago when Flying Saucer Revelations was first published in a very "primitive" format. We have not changed a word or comma. Let it help guide you to the "truth" about our visitors.

Tim Beckley, Publisher
MRUFO8@HOTMAIL.COM

FLYING SAUCER REVELATIONS

- by -

MICHAEL X

* * *

This is an Educational and Inspir-
ational Course of Study dealing with
Interplanetary subjects. It is especially written and intended   for
NEW AGE Individuals everywhere. The
following FIVE lessons are included
in this special Study:

1. "THE SAUCER PEOPLE ON EARTH"

2. "FLYING SAUCERS AT GIANT ROCK"

3. "SECRETS OF THE SAUCER PEOPLE"

4. "THE MAGIC OF ETHER SHIPS"

5. "DISCS, DESTINY AND YOU"

* * * * *

"FLYING SAUCER REVELATIONS" is based
on Scientific Findings, UFO data ac-
cumulated by numerous Researchers,
intensive Personal Investigation and
Mystical Revelation by the Author.

The Saucer People On Earth

by

MICHAEL X

Mystic Monograph No.1

Flying Saucer Revelations

"SAUCER PEOPLE ON EARTH"

Part One

Man's Secret Origin

Did you ever wonder about how you came to be on this planet? Where did you...and the other billions of human inhabitants of this Earth come from in the first place? What are the real facts?

You're going to be astounded and amazed when you find out the whole story of man's secret origin! You'll probably say to yourself "Why wasn't this information brought to my attention before?" and, "Why wasn't I taught this kind of knowledge in school, so I could have been making good use of it all these years? Why? Why? Why?

Well, for one thing, this is MYSTIC KNOWLEDGE. You can't expect to learn it in school, unless of course, it's a Mystic School. How many Mystic Schools are there? You can count them on the fingers on one hand. This is SECRET KNOWLEDGE. It's not commonly known at all. In fact, it is so rare and uncommon that as a general rule you have to search diligently for it, and "prove yourself" before it is revealed to you. That is why I'm going to give you certain facts-- some golden links in the chain of your GOOD--which have been so long withheld from you. I believe you are now ready for the great TRUTHS!

WHERE DID MAN   The fact is, Earthman is not the only tenant of
COME FROM ? ?   this universe. He only thinks he is. That is where
                    he makes a big mistake. There are countless other
Solar Systems throughout this vast universe in which highly intelligent human life forms are, at this very moment, living and breathing
the same as you and I! Many of those Systems are not merely hundreds
or thousands, but MILLIONS of years in advance of ours...and the
beings who inhabit those other "planetary chains" have a great deal
to do with YOUR secret origin.

According to many of the ancient teachings, ALL of the planets of this Solar System are inhabited by intelligent beings. Now I did not say PHYSICAL HUMAN BEINGS, such as are on Earth. It's might- ily important for you to realize that some of the planets in our System are peopled only by ETHERIC BEINGS. They don't have physical bodies like we do. But they do have a very efficient etheric body which they are very proud of, and which serves them nicely in many ways.
All beings--whether in physical or etheric form--are of course in varying grades of intelligence or "awareness of that which is". Each planet, for example, in our System is said to be actually a "School of Life" wherein the intelligent beings are able to learn certain vitally essential lessons in the true art of living.

Just as in any school, the idea is for all the individuals who dwell on any planet, to master the various "rules" or "laws" of life.

Flying Saucer Revelations

This is accomplished, of course, by learning how to consciously expand our awareness of the secret principles upon which your mind and your body and the entire universe are run.

When this is accomplished--and ONLY then--to the extent that an individual actually applies the knowledge he gains, he or she is permitted to "graduate" to another planet more advanced in the planetary scheme, where NEW LESSONS are learned. In this way, we progress from glory to glory...constantly unfolding our higher God-like powers!

Since there are a total of nine planets revolving around the Sun, it seems we Earthlings have Nine Schools to attend before we complete our "Course of Study" in this Solar System.

Each "School Term" lasts 2500 years. (Figuring in Cosmic Time this is not as long as you might think). At the end of that planetary cycle, some evolutionary cataclysm usually occurs (such as the Glacial Age, the Deluge, a Polar Shift, etc.) which, quite naturally, eliminates the "mass-minded" or the ones who "failed" in the earthly School of Life.

At the crucial time, however, some great Teacher of Light and Love appears on the planet. His purpose is to guide and direct the next class of intelligent beings who are arriving on the earthly scene for the first time. Jesus, Buddha, Zoroaster, Lao-Tse, Hermes Trismegistus, and Sanat Kumara (The Ancient of Days) were among the greatest of these Teachers. You could name many others.

What I am about to give you now is not new information. Rather, it is ages old. In fact, it is part of a body of Secret Knowledge that is called the Ageless Wisdom, for it is eternal. Some of this information is older than our planet itself(meaning it was given to us by higher intelligences from other planets and other systems.) Fortunately for you and me and other sincere Seekers, this marvelous body of knowledge has been preserved by a rare few of Earth's mystic masters in India, Tibet, Europe and America. The "Saucer Story" for instance, is an amazingly ancient story...known to certain advanced Earthlings for many, many centuries.

Before revealing the full story, I shall first "condition" your mind to several facts regarding interplanetary or space flight. The first thing to realize is that SPACE FLIGHT IS POSSIBLE. Our men of science on Earth now admit it. They believe that within the next ten years we shall have launched a rocket-ship to the moon and back. (They are even now experimenting in the building of our own "discs".)

This being so, what, I ask you, is there to have prevented some other planet, more highly advanced than our Earth, from having reached the same conclusion long ago. And, having reached such a definite conclusion, what is there to have stopped them from building a Space Ship in the logical form of a Flying Disc, and, using a better power than rocket power, conquering Space?!

Let us carry this thought a little further. Why do you think it is so difficult, so contrary to the thinking habits of our modern scientists to accept the idea that Flying Saucers already exist?

I will tell you why. If our "learned" scientists were to admit the existence of Spacecraft and Beings from other worlds, they would be admitting that our planet Earth is NOT the one and only planet in the Universe which has produced highly intelligent life forms. To admit such a thing would be a terrible blow to man's proud ego. It would force man to accept the fact that Earth is not the advanced place some of us think it is. Earth Man doesn't like to admit this.

The truth, according to ancient Hindu writings, is that Earth is but a "baby" in comparison to other planets in the universe. For example, Venus is one entire Chain (period of evolution) in advance of ours. Therefore, the intelligences of Venus are very highly evolved. This had to be, for the Venusian Race is ancient beyond belief in the sense that it originated many millions of years ago.

As for the story of the first consciously awakened Man on Earth, it really begins in the year 18,617,841 B.C. In other words, the date of our epic is eighteen million, six hundred and seventeen thousand, eight hundred and forty-one years before the birth of Christ.

In that momentous year--as revealed by ancient Hindu writings-- the first space ship came from the planet Venus, to land here on planet Earth. From Venus, "The Home of the Gods", came Sanat Kumara, (The Lord of the Flame) with his four Great Lords and one hundred assistants. These shining beings saw to it that human souls became incarnated in physical bodies on Earth.

Until the arrival on Earth of Sanat Kumara from Venus, Man did not have conscious awareness. He was the product of long ages of slow evolving upon planet Earth. Physically he resembled Man as we know him today; but mentally he was like the animals. That is, he lived only in his subconsciousness. The front section of his brain was asleep.

When the Lord of the Flame saw the poor mindless thing that was Man, he felt moved to assist directly in Man's unfoldment. He used his spiritual powers to awaken the centers of individuality in the Earth Man.

This fact is the "missing link" in the evolution of Man on this planet.

The Lord Sanat Kumara called the first consciously awakened man Adam, in tribute to the Venusian Lords who belonged to the Adamic Race of Venus. At the time of his conscious awakening, Adam's body was androgynous or bi-sexual. He was a two-fold being, having both male and female components perfectly balanced within his own physical body. To facilitate the propagation of offspring, Sanat Kumara changed the sex polarity of Adam from bi-sexual to uni-sexual. This led to the creation of Eve who became Adam's mate.

Adam and Eve were blessed with children and the Adamic line

branched out to cover the entire face of the globe. All of us here on Earth--regardless of color, or of "belief-conditioning"--are direct descendants of Adam and Eve; and indirect descendants of the Adamic Race of Venus.

After Sanat Kumara and his helpers had finished their work of starting a physical race of Mankind on Earth, they returned again to Venus and left man to evolve higher up the ladder of Life through his own personal efforts and illuminating experiences. It was only right that the Lord Thinkers should leave Man then, for those brilliant Beings belonged to an entirely different Life Chain than ours.

As the centuries of time rolled by, men of Earth learned many secrets of universal power, secrets which most people of today believe to be strictly modern and "new" discoveries of science. The hidden truth however, is that what we call new is "old stuff" to the Saucer People of the inhabited planets in space. They've been masters of a "Secret Science" of the universe which is so ancient its origin is lost in the mists of time. Some of their truths are not millions, but billions and trillions of years old. Much of the knowledge has been passed from one planet to another, such as the "formula" for successful Space Flight, De-Gravitation, Telethot, etc. etc. There simply is nothing essentially NEW under the sun; though our modern science likes to think so.

As Man's "I.Q." increased, wonderful civilizations such as those on Atlantis, Lemuria and Mu, were built,..but each time they fell apart or were destroyed chiefly through misuse of their own great powers. In addition to the calamitous results of human foolishness, Nature itself rebelled many times. Great planetary cataclysms occurred, due to a sudden shifting of the poles of the Earth. The Great Deluge, or Flood, was one of these. It is important, because it is part of the whole amazing story of Flying Saucers, the Space People, who they are and what their seemingly "mysterious" purpose really is.

Way back in the days of Noah, the Earth shifted its poles. At once a monstrous Tidal Wave swept over all of the then populated areas of the world, destroying nearly all living beings. All the marvelous ancient records, manuscripts, secrets, etc., were lost to mankind, and man was forced to begin again his long upward climb toward the Light. Did I say ALL was lost? Not quite all. We must not forget the fabulous "Bible in Stone"--THE GREAT PYRAMID OF EGYPT! Let us now see how the Great Pyramid "ties in" to the picture.

Shortly before the Noaic Deluge took place, the Saucer People had realized that such a disaster was impending. They could tell, from their observations made in space, that the Earth was about to SHIFT POSITION. In the short time remaining before the "shift" was to occur, the Saucer People--Venusians--went into positive action on behalf of humanity's present and future welfare. The Lords of Venus determined to build an "altar to the Lord in the midst of the land of Egypt, and a pillar at the border thereof to the Lord. And it shall be for a SIGN and for a WITNESS unto the Lord of Hosts in the land of Egypt."--Isaiah 19:19-20.

Flying Saucer Revelations

You no doubt are aware that the Great Pyramid was designed by beings of extraordinary intelligence. The perfect knowledge of Astronomy revealed by the Pyramid was "first-hand" knowledge possessed by those Masters of Space and Time, the Lords of Venus!

Inner teaching has it that the Lord Thinkers directed one of Earth's wisest mortals, King Thothmus, as to HOW the entire edifice was to be constructed. Thothmus was a great mystic, and cooperated fully with the Venusians for he understood that the building of the Great Pyramid would serve FIVE vital purposes:

      1. To preserve Secret Knowledge on Earth.
      2. To prophesy the future of Earthmen.
      3. To serve as a Temple of Mystic Truth.
      4. To be a SIGN or landmark for Space Ships.
      5. To be a WITNESS unto the Lord of Hosts.

As you know, certain principles of construction were used which are still the wonder of the world, even today. For instance, so accurately were the stones interlocked in the Pyramid that you can scarcely insert a calling card between the blocks, today.

The "Lord of Hosts" refers to that highly evolved and mighty being, Jesus Christ, whose kingdom was of "another world" ("not of this world")....a planet in our Solar System that is far ahead of us in spiritual unfoldment. This highly spiritual soul was be be born on Earth, and become an outstanding Teacher of Light and Love.

So the Pyramid was built and the Knowledge of Ages concealed within its stone walls, to endure down through the centuries. Noah, a sincere seeker of spiritual Light, was contacted by the Saucer People and warned of the planetary shifting that was soon to destroy the Men of Planet 3 (Earth). So Noah built an Ark as directed.

THEN THE EARTH SHOOK TERRIBLY!

And the oceans ROARED over the land, flooding ALL of the populated areas. "And the waters prevailed exceedingly upon the Earth; and all the high hills, that were under the whole heaven, were covered. Fifteen cubits upward did the waters prevail; and the MOUNTAINS were covered. And ALL FLESH DIED that moved upon the Earth, both of fowl, and of cattle, and of beast, and of every creeping thing upon the Earth, and EVERY MAN. All in whose nostrils was the breath of life, of ALL that was in the dry land, died."--Genesis 7:19.

NOAH and his few faithful followers were, of course, spared... so that the Race could continue as the Lord Thinkers had planned. And so it has continued to this day.

Only one thing is wrong. Some of us Earthlings, too many of us, in fact, have refused to grow as fast in the spiritual department of life as we have grown in the mental, technical and material phases of living. How very deplorable! We've been told time and time again, "With all thy getting, get understanding!" That means SPIRITUAL WISDOM does it not? What do you think our nation, in fact our whole

Flying Saucer Revelations

world NEEDS most right now? More Guided Rocket Missiles? More Super-Sonic Jet Bombers? More A-Bombs and H-Bombs in our "stock-pile"?

No. A million times NO! You know the answer as well as I. We need a dynamic SPIRITUAL AWAKENING! We need to send out a great LOVE-RAY to our fellowman in every country, and lift him up into a higher kind of "response". But in order to send out such a Love-Ray we must ourselves, individually as well as collectively, feel and experience this dynamic SPIRITUAL AWAKENING. We must cease smothering our spiritual wisdom. We must refuse to let it be choked out by the wasted attentions we give to matters which are NOT Spiritual. Only the true LOVE-RAY(which our Greatest of Teachers explained to us 2,000 years ago) can nullify the effect of the horrible DEATH-RAY that man keeps "tinkering" with.

THE AIR FORCE NOW BUILDS OWN FLYING SAUCERS. The Department of Defense in our country just recently released a most interesting report, prepared by the United States Air Force. It stated that a new type of "vertical rising, DISC-shaped aircraft is now being built for the Air Force by AVRO, Ltd., Canada. Why build a Flying Saucer? For several good reasons. It can take off vertically without any need of a large landing field. Once it is in horizontal flight, it will be capable of enormous SPEED.

Soon you'll be seeing plenty of "Saucers" in the sky, produced by Earthmen, if the AVRO project turns out successfuly. We hope it works out for them, for we understand they've poured six million dollars into the project already. Back in 1945 the Air Force did not put much "stock" in the real "existence" of Flying Discs, even when the Discs were buzzing all around Washington, D. C., the seat of our Government.

In the Air Force report, which you can read in the April 1956 issue of Fantasy and Science Fiction magazine (on your newsstands or send 35¢ to Fantasy House, Inc. 471 Park Ave., New York 22, N. Y.)--the findings of their "Saucer Investigations" during the past three years are--to our way of thinking--still very"inconclusive". The idea of an extra-terrestial origin of the "Unidentified Aerial Objects" is carefully avoided.

Authorities can sometimes be quite misleading. Perhaps for a valid reason, such as "security" measures, or to avert public panic. We can understand this. But let us, you and I, think for ourselves with the evidence before us. The real Truth about the Discs, the landing of the Saucer People on Earth, and their vital mission, will thus be revealed to us by our own "Knower" within!

This "Knower" within is the revealer of all true wisdom and can be contacted by keeping your attention upon the Great True Self, or God-Presence within your own heart. It is only by devotion to this spiritual center within you that the "Knower" reveals true wisdom. The wisest men who ever lived on earth attained wisdom in this way!

* * * * *

A PERSONAL NOTE

The Truth is never
impossible; merely
incredible. When we
expand our personal
awareness beyond the
norm, all of Life's
"mysteries" vanish.
They become new
truths made plain!
Happily, Truth is no
respecter of persons.
That is why Visitors
from Space have made
contact with Earth-
lings from many diff-
erent walks of life.
Let us now consider
some of those contacts,
and discover what they
mean to you, to me, and
to all the people of
Earth.

                    THE AUTHOR

Flying Saucer Revelations

"SAUCER PEOPLE ON EARTH"

Part Two

The Contacts

The average person still is inclined to consider the subject of "Flying Saucers" as a huge joke. Mention the words to your next door neighbor and you will instantly know, from the reaction you get, what I mean.

That is regrettable. Flying Saucers are in no sense a joking matter. Flying Saucers are REALITIES. Interplanetary flight is a REALITY. And the Saucer People are also living REALITIES. I wish I could make these points even more emphatic. The time for joking is past. We must learn the true facts and the real meaning of the Saucers. And we must accept the facts for what they are.

NON-TERRESTIAL   Literally millions of people on earth have sighted
ORIGIN OF THE   Spacecraft. In fact, they have been seen by earth-
FLYING SAUCERS.   lings for countless centuries, and so recorded by
                        astronomers and historians of all races and coun-
tries on Earth. All attempts to "debunk" the existence of the Flying Saucers in no way invalidates the authentic facts, carefully gathered from all over the world, which PROVE that Unidentified Flying Objects of amazing character, and of a non-terrestial origin have been, and still are being seen.

Let's go backwards a bit in time to the year 1519. The place, Old Mexico. The Aztec Indians, under the rule of Montezuma, were in their glory. They had conquered most of the country, were rich and powerful. But they practiced HUMAN SACRIFICE to an extent never equalled by any race in the history of the world. This was something directly contrary to all the laws of the Space People (as well as to the law of their own great teacher, Quetzal-Coatl).

In order to end the evil practice and disperse the powerful Aztecs forever, the "Lord Thinkers" sent a series of mysterious and frightening "omens" to the king Montezuma. Omens included a predic- tion of the exact date on which the white men under Cortes, would conquer the Aztecs. A vision of the future gathered from the land of the dead by Montezuma's sister. And lastly, brilliant lights in the night sky. Let me describe those "lights" more fully.

On the eastern horizon of Mexico appeared a tremendously large, brightly glowing object shaped somewhat like a triangle. It was so brilliant that it lighted up the whole countryside and could be seen from midnight till dawn for a period of FORTY DAYS!

Another strange omen was the mysterious "disintegration" of two stone temples (in which human sacrifice was performed) by some power- ful ray coming from the Spaceship which hovered overhead. An account of all these happenings can be found in the ancient history books and legends of Old Mexico, showing that Saucers are not NEW.

Flying Saucer Revelations

Now let us move swiftly up to more modern times to the year 1952...to be precise, the night of July 29, 1952. The place, Miami Florida. There had been a flurry of "sightings" of Flying Saucers in the Miami Area during both June and July, so one young U. S. Marine photographer (now out of uniform) was alert and ready with his movie camera to "catch" a Saucer on film. PIC Magazine for June 1954, printed an article by Ralph Mayher, the determined young photographer who proved on film that Flying Saucers are REAL.

Mr. Mayher's movie film lasted a full three minutes. It showed a glowing, disc-like object in motion, which became closer and brighter in each frame of the picture. It moved with an incredible speed. How fast? Ralph Mayher sent his movie film to the University of Florida physics department for a calculated report.

7550 miles per hour...was their figure! That's at least 5550 miles per hour FASTER than any of our high-speed super-sonic jets! In his letter reporting the calculated speed of the object, the assistant Professor of Physics at the University expressed his belief that the "saucer" did not travel at this high speed for the full three minutes. Rather, it came into sight at a much SLOWER speed, then accelerated into tremendous velocity and sped away.

If our own world's fastest Guided Missiles are only capable of travelling at a speed of around 2,000 miles an hour; then isn't it only logical that these "U.F.O's" have an interplanetary origin... and do NOT originate here on this Earth at all?

Time: February, 1956. Place: Alameda County near San Francisco. Sargent Larry White of the Alameda County office saw some spectacular purplish "lights" in the sky, as he glanced up from his patrol car on Stonybrook road near Decoto. The lights were gigantic in size and could be seen for nearly 45 minutes between clouds. They looked like giant "railroad flairs" to Sargent White and others. The San Francisco newspapers carried the story next day.

Saucers are today's biggest "mystery". That is, they are a mystery to those whose minds are tightly closed against the Truth. But the Truth about Flying Saucers has been with us for "lo, these many years." You need only seek and you will be astounded.

The Bible mentions them many times. It refers to them as the "fiery chariots of the Lord". Listen to this sentence from Isaiah 66:15, "For behold, the Lord will come with fire, and with his chariots..." And read Psalm 68:17, "The chariots of God are twenty thousand..." And do not overlook 2nd Kings, 2:11. It says, "Will he return from heaven as he went, by a whirlwind, and in a chariot of fire?" Aren't these "chariots" merely another way of describing the objects that Kenneth Arnold named "Flying Saucers"?

Ezekiel gives this fascinating account of Flying Saucers in Chapter 1:16 of the Bible. "The appearance of the Wheels and their work was like unto the color of a beryl (bluish green stone) and their appearance and their work was as it were a wheel in the middle of a wheel." (NOTE: Read all of Chapt. 1 of Exekiel.)

Flying Saucer Revelations

The fact is, Flying Saucers are continually appearing in greater numbers in different parts of the world (France, Russia, Mexico, England, Australia, as well as the United States). The question is, why? Whence do they come? and what do they want?

The inhabitants of other planets (both the etheric and physical people who live on other worlds) realize that we Earthlings have the atomic bomb and the even worse Hydrogen bomb. They know that all-out atomic warfare on Earth could wipe out the race of Man almost overnight. It could also have dire effects on the entire universe, since all things interact in the great Cosmic Scheme.

Not only might the Earthlings--in their stupidity--succeed in blowing themselves to bits; but they might also affect seriously the etheric regions which surround our planet and its stratosphere. The Etherean Beings certainly have no intention of permitting such an etheric disaster to occur. Not if they can prevent it.

On at least a dozen occasions, the Space People have been known to land their Spacecraft and converse with people of Earth. And... at least eight persons from our Earth have assertedly been aboard their ships and had enlightening talks with the Saucerians. Three persons, Dan Frey, George Van Tassel, and Orfeo Angelucci, assert they have not only been aboard a Space Ship; but have enjoyed an actual RIDE in the amazing craft.

On August 24th of 1953, George Van Tassel of Giant Rock in Yucca Valley, California, was wakened out of his sleep around 2 A.M. The strange visitor who stood before him at the foot of his bed spoke to him, saying: "My name is Solgonda. I would be pleased to show you our craft."

"From the time I got out of bed, until I returned to it," says George, "Every time I thought of something to say he was answering me before I could speak the first word of any sentence. This proved to me their perfect ability to communicate by Thought Transference."

As they approached the Ship, George began to get "butterflies" in his stomach from about fifty feet away. On getting nearer, his hair seemed to want to stand up on end. (NOTE: Magnetic force-fields of great strength can create this effect.)

On entering the Space Ship the feeling immediately disappeared. Solgonda showed George around the Ship, demonstrating the various instruments used for celestial space navigation. Even the "engine" was seen clearly enough so that George could mentally grasp something of the advanced principle by which it operated. After about 20 minutes of sheer elation to say nothing of revelation, George was accompanied by Solgonda back to George's bed and the strange visitation was terminated.

What do these "contacts" tell us" Many things...strange to us and wonderful. Firstly, the beings from space are NOT warlike.

Flying Saucer Revelations

If they were, we'd have been annihilated centuries ago. No, they are here to help...not harm us. In fact, the very laws of the universe by which they live will not permit them to harm us. It is through helping Earth Man to understand life, and his right relation to the Cosmos and his fellow beings, that the "Lord Thinkers" of other worlds advance themselves in the great scheme of things!

Remember the planetary "Schools of Life". They are governed by a simple rule. The closer a planet is to the center of a given Solar System, that is, its Sun, the more intense LIGHT it receives from that Sun. The higher also are its spiritual vibrations. In other words, the inhabitants of such a planet are <u>filled</u> <u>with</u> <u>light</u> hence are more highly intelligent and spiritual.

Conversely, the farther away a planet is from its Sun, the less LIGHT its inhabitants are able to receive. Thus they are proportionately less intelligent and less spiritual than bodies nearer the Sun. By "spiritual" we mean EN-LIGHT-ENED, or more powerfully charged with the light frequency which carries the "desire" or the "will" of the One Great Light that runs the Cosmos.

Mercury is that orb nearer to the Sun than any other of the planets in our System. It is number One in order. Next in line of distance from our Sun is Venus. The next is planet Earth. Next is Mars, then Jupiter, etc., etc. This would put Venus one planetary Round ahead of us, and the planet Mercury two Rounds in advance of us. Mars, then, would be behind us in spiritual evolution or Enlightenment.

HOW TO SIGHT A "SAUCER". Flying Saucers have been sighted so universally that it is entirely possible that you might be fortunate enough to sight one or more of them in your own vicinity. I would recommend sincerely that you secure for yourself a small telescope, or at least a good pair of binoculars or "opera-glasses". (I never travel without them in my car). Carry them with you on your person every time you go to the nearby hills, desert or beach resort.

My technique for sighting Flying Saucers is basically similar to that used by such notables as George Adamski of Mount Palomar, George Van Tassel of Giant Rock, Truman Bethurum, and others. Here is the essence of the method, which I recommend to you:

1. Get away from large cities. There is so much light and atmospheric disturbance around big cities, it's practically impossible to detect any Saucer phenomena in the skies. Try to spend a full weekend in the country or on the desert. Your chances of sighting a disc will thereby be increased many fold.

2. Don't try to see Spacecraft during mid-day. Sunlight makes them almost invisible. Wait until afternoon or evening or night before scanning the skies. You might even prefer to hold your "Saucer Vigil" all night long, then sleep during the daytime. Remember, they glow at night (often resembling a full moon of reddish orange color) so you will be able to spot them quickly if they should happen to cross the sky in your vicinity.

Flying Saucer Revelations

3. If at all possible, go where the Flying Saucers are reported to have been seen by other people whom you believe to be reliable. This would be primarily the desert areas of California, Arizona, New Mexico etc., as these make the most ideal natural landing places.

4. Form a definite habit of following your inner feelings. Let the gentle voice of Intuition lead you to the proper place where a genuine sighting of a Flying Saucer can be made. Follow all leads.

5. Be persistent. Numerous trips to various localities might be necessary before you are rewarded with the amazing view you are now seeking. On the other hand, YOU may be one of the fortunate individuals who might not only see an interplanetary Spaceship but contact the beings within it also...and all this when you least expect it!

6. Do not be skeptical. This mental attitude cuts you off from the desirable attractive state of mind that is essential to success. Be open-minded. So many sightings are on record now by qualified observers, very little "blind faith" is required. With sightings now increasing instead of decreasing, your chances of personally seeing a "UFO" are getting better and better.

7. Familiarize yourself with the various kinds of sky objects that are most commonly mistaken for Flying Saucers but actually are not. These include (a) Weather balloons, (b) High altitude balloons or "Sky Hooks", (c) New type aircraft, (d) Unusual cloud effects. By knowing what these and other natural sky phenomena look like, you will be able to refute any arguments by "Saucer Critics" who may try to belittle your sightings by claiming you are not "up" on the new developments in Aviation and Science. This information will also enable you to recognize a genuine UFO when you see one. Remember too that the regular habit of looking upward "to the sky" will so strengthen your vision you will be able to see higher and farther.

You have only to see a single one of these amazing Spacecraft to know forevermore that they are not illusion, delusion, nor merely imagination. Nor are they simply "spots before the eyes" as some persons would have us believe. It is my conviction that Flying Saucers do exist and all men will see them in the Golden Age coming. In this monograph I have given you many vital links in the seeming mystery of Flying Saucers. If you follow the suggestions I have given you will be rewarded, in a wonderful way. Be bold. Intuitively, you KNOW flying saucers exist. All that remains is for you to sight one (or several at once) for yourself.

To you then will come a glorious NEW consciousness--an ecstatic feeling of dwelling in two different worlds at one time. This feeling will persist with you for days after your first sighting of an interplanetary craft. As a final closing word now I would remind you that sincere desire is in reality PRAYER. So if you wholeheartedly desire to sight a Flying Saucer, in due time you shall. It may not be tomorrow, but the day will come. When it happens, it will be one of the most thrilling days you've ever known on planet Earth!

oooOOOooo

Flying Saucer Revelations

Flying Saucers At Giant Rock

by

MICHAEL X

Mystic Monograph No. 2

Flying Saucer Revelations

"FLYING SAUCERS AT GIANT ROCK"

Part One

Out of This World.

Dr. Nephi Cottam gazed in amazement at the glittering, glowing, silvery thing hovering motionless in the sky above him. He had never seen a space ship before. He was seeing one now, and he knew it.

The "Saucer" was about two miles above the ground. It had not been there a minute ago. Now, however, it was there and...it was REAL. Nephi had no doubt about that.

He had spotted the Flying Saucer a few seconds before, when it first appeared. Then it was only a tiny spot of bright light in the far distance; but as he watched in complete fascination, the "light" seemed to hurl itself across the miles of sky until it reached its present position. There it rested quietly above the crowd below.

Nephi smiled. It was really true. He was seeing a Flying Saucer. It wasn't merely "imagination", nor was it a case of having "spots before the eyes". That bright circular object in the sky was every bit as much of a reality to him as was the light bulb in his bedroom lamp at home. If that light bulb was "real", so was this Saucer. He turned to the man next to him.

"What does that look like to you?" Nephi asked.

"Flying Saucer!" the other man said.

"Yes," Nephi remarked, "It's a Saucer."

But then, that's exactly what he had been hoping to see. That is what several thousand other people at this meeting had been hoping to see. Now they were happily sighting a ship from another world.

It was the exciting climax to a never-to-be-forgotten day at Giant Rock Airport in Yucca Valley, California. The date was Sunday, March 12, 1955. The latest interplanetary Spacecraft Convention was going on, and people from all walks of life were on hand for the tremendous occasion.

George Adamski, author of "Flying Saucers Have Landed", was a guest speaker. So was Frank Scully ("Behind the Flying Saucers"), Orfeo Angelucci and Truman Bethurum--who have been aboard the space-ships--were also there. George W. Van Tassel, author of the start-ling book, "I Rode a Flying Saucer", was another of the many notable Saucer authorities who were present at the Convention.

It was late afternoon. Nephi looked up again. The Saucer was still motionless and silent like a flashlight in the sky. There

were no clouds to obscure it from view. All you had to do now
was look up and you would see it. Those intelligent beings up there
certainly knew what was going on down here at the "Rock"; but in
spite of the fact that this Convention was "in their honor", they
made no attempt to land their glowing Space Ship.

All at once, the Saucer accelerated suddenly, then went straight
up higher and higher until finally it was lost to view. The crowd
began dispersing, for the "show" was over and tomorrow was a workday.
Nephi Cottam returned to his home in Los Angeles.

When I talked with him a month later, the memory of having
"sighted" an actual Flying Saucer was still fresh and clear in his
mind. Since I had not been able to attend the Spacecraft Convention
myself, I got as complete an account of the event as I wanted, from
Nephi. I have known the doctor for a number of years. He is the
originator of a unique and wonderful method of healing known as
"Craniopathy". This is a technique for releasing Brain-Energy by
physical and mental means.

Past experience has proven Nephi to be a remarkable individual.
Through meditation and intuitive insight, he has gained access to
healing knowledge which, if the world knew about it, would largely
do away with the need for "going to doctors". The individual would
merely apply a sort of "Self-Therapy" and remain ever healthy.

Nephi Cottam was working for the good of mankind, along the
lines of Truth. So there was no reason for me to doubt his integ-
rity. All that I needed was more facts.

My personal knowledge of Giant Rock Airport and the men and
women who lived at the "Rock" was, at the moment, rather sketchy.
I knew only that the "man in charge" at Giant Rock was one George W.
Van Tassel. It was my impression that George operated a private
Airport there in Yucca Valley, and was a licensed airplane pilot.
Also, I was aware that George had written an account of his "contact"
with the Space People, and the ride he had in one of their inter-
planetary "Air Ships". That, in a nutshell, was all I knew about the
mysterious activities of "George's Group" at Giant Rock. Remember,
I had never been there.

It seemed to me, however, that George Van Tassel was one person
who understood some things about Flying Saucers that most people
(including yours truly) didn't know. If George was actually in personal contact with the Saucer People, then he logically must have
received certain information from them which to us would be tremendously vital. Reasoning along these lines, I concluded that a "Field
trip" to Giant Rock was in order. I asked Nephi if he could join me.

"Surely," he replied, "How about leaving Los Angeles at six
A. M. on May the 8th?"

Flying Saucer Revelations

"Fine, I agreed. An early start was always a good idea. It was quite a distance out to the desert from the city center. Then too, we planned to return to L.A. in the evening of the same day if all went well.

On Sunday morning, 8 May, we drove to Giant Rock. By taking the Super Highways which had recently been completed between L.A. and San Bernardino, the trip to Yucca Valley--although more than a hundred miles--seemed like a "breeze" to us. Almost before we knew it, the dry desert land was stretching out in front of us. Soon we found ourselves bumping over an unpaved dirt road in the direction of the private Airport. The terrain became more scenic. Instead of uninteresting flat desert, huge rocks and boulders of all sizes lay scattered about.

Nephi pointed to a small sign at an intersection in the road. It read, "Giant Rock Airport". We followed it. Abruptly we came to another sign which said, "George's Gang Welcomes You". Then we saw the "Rock". Several "stories" in height, Giant Rock was aptly named. I sensed the immensity , the strength and majesty of its presence. Although no match in size for the famous Rock of Gibralter, Giant Rock was, for all that, quite a "pebble" in its own right.

As we drove up to the base of the Rock, a man approaced in response to my friendly greeting and wave of the hand. He was a well-proportioned, intelligent looking individual. I mentally catalogued him as a sturdy "salt of the earth" Dutchman.

We introductd ourselves, and the man smiled pleasantly. "I'm George Van Tassel" he said. "Make yourselves at home, and I will show you about in a few minutes."

I parked at one side of the Rock. We got out, stretched, then looked around. Not many other people in sight. Maybe a "baker's dozen" or so, including us two. There was, I realized, no "Convention" of any kind going on now. That, in a way, was fortunate for us. There would be no swarming crowds of people all trying to talk to George at the same time. He would have more time to converse with us.

George invited us into one of the few small buildings located close to the Rock. It was designed to serve as a "short-order" Cafe, for the conveniences of visitors. Behind the counter stood a woman, whom George introduced as his wife. The walls of the cafe were covered with photographs and drawings of spaceships of every description. I stepped over to them, noting all details as carefully as possible. One of the pictures showed a great cloud shaped liked a huge bowl, hovering about a half mile above the earth. It was clear that the "cloud" was more than it appeared to be. George explained to us:

"That is actually a Saucer camouflaging itself within its own force field of energy. To our physical eye it looks like a large, swirling cloud."

Flying Saucer Revelations

I glanced quickly at several of the other pictures. A number of them bore the name and copyright notice of George Adamski. There were the well known photos of saucers passing between the earth and the moon, with the moon in the background. Also, telescopic pictures of a giant carrier ship, often called the "mother ship". It was shaped like a cigar. The pictures were amazing.

George seemed interested in us. He began answering some of our questions. When he spoke, you got the impression he was speaking from personal experience. Everything he said fitted together like links in a chain. Nothing seemed to perturb him.

"Are the Saucers interplanetary?" I asked, "Or do they come from some Government on Earth?"

"They come from other planets," George said. "Mainly from Venus. Scientists on Earth have not captured the secret of inter-stellar travel, which is simply based upon use of FREE Energy. The Space People have found out how to channel that power."

"FREE Energy," I remarked, "Isn't that what Walter Russell was talking about in his book called "The Secret of Light?"

"Yes, there is a very good description of the secondary effects of Light in that book. Light is really the basic Universal Power. It passes constantly through your body, maintaining life. It causes planets to spin, nebulae to evolve, suns to shine, and really runs the whole universe."

Nephi and I both nodded our heads to show that the idea made sense to us. We felt ourselves to be on the verge of some truly tremendous discoveries about Life.

"FREE Energy," continued George, "is Free. That's where the rub comes. Imagine, no more light bills to pay nor gasoline to buy. No more special money interests. All you can use would be free. They can't patent the power that runs the Cosmos! Everyone would be using FREE Energy. It's so simple any good mechanic can make the equipment for utilizing it in a million ways!"

"That would upset our world economy," I commented, "Imagine, no money system!"

"Authorities are trying hard to prevent the inevitable from hap-pening," George said, "That's why they're hiding their findings about Flying Saucers. They are mortally afraid that the public will find out about the FREE Energy that powers the universe!"

It was easy to see that the "FREE Energy" was a bombshell of no little proportions. No wonder the real facts were being kept hidden from the man in the street. The story of Keely's motor flashed to mind. I recalled that John Worrell Keely, a lonely inventor of Philadelphia, Penna., had developed a motor which generated its own power after having once been started. If allowed to continue running it would do so until the bearings wore themselves out!

What happened to Keely's engine? It had one disadvantage. Unless Keely himself was there the engine would not operate. So the money-backers lost interest, and Keely faded into obscurity, a disillusioned man.

Nikola Tesla, the famed wizard of electricity, also stumbled onto the secret of FREE Energy. He built a working model of an engine, to demonstrate a simple form of perpetual motion. Money-interests got wind of it, however, and wrecked his laboratory.

Bell Telephone Company recently developed a "Solar Battery" consisting of a series of flat crystals which store up energy from the sun. Though crude, this is a step in the right direction of FREE Energy.

I do not doubt that the secret will be rediscovered and used again by man to speed his spiritual progress. Occultists are now aware of the basic principle: Intercept the lines of light energy from the sun, and you bring about a rotation movement. This is how planets revolve. Motors do likewise.

"Would you care to see our room under the Rock?" George asked us. We assured him that we would be happy to accompany him there. I had a hunch that much more knowledge was about to be revealed.

* * * * * *

Flying Saucer Revelations

"FLYING SAUCERS AT GIANT ROCK"

Part Two

"Wisdom of The Cosmos"

It was midafternoon. The desert sky was intensely clear and
blue. The air was fresh and exhilarating. Dr. Nephi Cottam and I
followed in single file behind George Van Tassel as he walked out of
the "Cafe" toward the "Communications Room" underneath Giant Rock.

George opened a door leading down a series of stone steps into
the "Room". It was a spacious place, and gave me the eerie feeling
of being inside solid rock. The ceiling of the Room, however, con-
sisted of a small portion of the bottom of the Rock. The builders
had dug under one edge of the Rock, scraped out space for a room,
then built up walls around it.

Other visitors to the Rock--ten or so in number--joined us as
we descended the stone stairs into the Room below. Several chairs
were available there, so all of us sat down in a semicircle around
the main speaker, which of course, was George.

He began speaking, and we listened.

"The scientists of Earth are majoring in the science of destruction, in separation, disintegration and taking things apart. According to the Space People, that is the wrong approach to the mysteries
of Creation.

"We, as a people, shall only attain supreme Knowledge and the
wisdom of the Cosmos by constructive efforts, by putting things
together. Our science is in error.

"Nuclear energy--atomic power--is being used so negatively that
our whole planet is endangered. Every explosion brings about a
reaction in the lines of force maintaining planetary balance or
equilibrium. Each explosion charges our atmosphere with radioactive
debris that will remain poisonous for thousands of years.

"The Space People are aware of these dangers and, for the sake
of humanity on this planet as well as the life on other worlds, are
seeking to nullify the effects."

One of the group had a question: "What do the Space People
look like? I heard that they are smaller than we are."

"Yes, they are 'Little People' when they come from a planet
with a gravitational density greater than ours," George said.

"On the other hand, many planets have produced beings of our
average size. Some Solar Systems beyond ours produce people whom
you or I would consider to be giants.

Flying Saucer Revelations

"The teaching of the Church is that there is only a 'here' and a 'hereafter'. Here means of course, the earth. Hereafter refers to Heaven or to Purgatory, a place where souls wait to be let into Heaven. All such dogma is wrong because it seeks to limit the Creator. It tries to confine God to only two life levels, whereas the fact is that people are coming to our level (Earth) in space-craft from many different levels throughout the Cosmos.

"'In my Father's House are many mansions', Jesus reminded us. Substitute the word 'planets' for 'mansions' and you get a much clearer picture of what he meant.

"Visitors from space have told us that they have found human life everywhere. On many planets in other Solar Systems the people are advanced so far beyond us earthlings in Culture and Science, it staggers the imagination. We of Earth simply can't comprehend how anybody could be more 'advanced' and 'intelligent' than we are.

"But what are the facts? Is not the whole economy of the nations of Earth based on manufacturing weapons of destruction, planes, jets, guided missiles, battleships, tanks, and atomic or hydrogen bombs? Take away the iron fist of the Military and the nation would, supposedly, be doomed."

At this point George paused briefly. He seemed to be waiting for another question from the group. I gave him one.

"Why are the Saucers coming to our Earth?" I asked, "Is something big impending?"

I had known for some time that Flying Saucers have been landing on Earth in continually greater numbers. What did this mean? What did the Saucer People want? I felt that George might supply the key.

"A planetary cataclysm of Terra (the Earth) has been foreseen by the Space People," George said. "At the present time we are not only on the pinnacle of a Minor Cycle, which is approximately every 2100 years, but are also in the middle of a Major or Master Cycle (about 26,000 years) at the same time. This brings about a balancing of the planetary forces.

"In the Christian Bible this is called the time of the great earthquake, or the 'shaking terribly' of the earth. (For the full story, see Monograph No. 5.)

"According to the Space People, that is the time when a 'polar flip' will occur, due to the gyroscopic action of the earth. When this event takes place, many of Earth's inhabitants will be taken out of physical embodiment. These will be the mass-minded who have no interest in matters of a spiritual or cosmic nature.

"The other people of Earth—those who have diligently sought the 'Light' and endeavored to become better human beings—will be taken up in Flying Saucers by the Space People, and protected by them until the planetary catastrophe is over.

"Then," continued George, "the 'elect' will be returned to Earth to bring in the Millenium, the thousand years of peace."

This, I recalled, tied in with the Biblical prophecies of the 'last days' in which John foretold of a "new heaven and a new Earth". This new Earth would be under the law of the spirit, which is the "New Dispensation" mankind has long awaited. "And God shall wipe away all tears from their eyes; and there shall be no more death, neither sorrow, nor crying, neither shall there be any more pain: for the former things are passed away." (Rev. Chapter 21:4)

The idea of our Earth making a sudden 'shift' of its axis at periodic intervals, has long been known to Occultists. Those who study the ancient teachings of man--the Ageless Wisdom--have long been aware of "Cataclysmic Cycles" which occur regularly in the history of most planets.

There is, in fact, a definite pattern of periodic "destruction", which is Nature's own doing. As you know, each planet begins its human life expression with what is called a "Root Race". Each Root Race lasts for about 5 million years, then is almost completely annihilated by either water or fire. Then the next Root Race begins, from a small nucleus of persons who were spared.

It is said that each planet of our Solar System is allowed to have 7 Root Races. (I am not speaking now of the white race, colored race, yellow race, etc., but rather the Race of Man itself). We of this day and age are members of the 5th Root Race.

Root races of odd number are subject to destruction by fire. This, in modern times could mean not only physical fire as we know it, but could include the Hydrogen Bomb which creates a holocaust of flames. Strangely enough, if we look backwards for a moment to note how the previous Root Races perished, we see the following: The first Root Race--the Adamic--was cut in two by a "fiery sword", which drove Adam and Eve out of the Garden of Eden. This "fiery sword" was in reality a fiery comet that approached too close to planet Earth and became drawn into our terrestial atmosphere. The comet with its "tail of fire" looked much like a burning sword of vengeance.

The second Root Race (a Sub-Race of the first) was undoubtedly the Noaic Race, or Noah and his people. As you realize, most of the human race in the time of Noah were a bad lot, having lost sight of their own spiritual heritage. Noah, of course, was the exception; hence he and his faithful followers were spared when the Deluge came.

Ancient writings tell us that Lemuria became the third Root Race after the Deluge. Volcanic disturbances of the Earth caused such upheavals of the oceans that the continent of Lemuria was swept over by the Pacific Ocean...wiping out most of the Race.

Flying Saucer Revelations

The Fourth Race Atlanteans, we learn, met a watery fate at the bottom of the Atlantic.

According to the Great Pyramid, we are now living in the Saturday Night of Time. It is, actually, the beginning of the "Time of the End" for humankind on Earth. This means that some collossal changes are due to take place before January 1, 2,000 A.D.

There is, however, no need for panic. So far as you and I are concerned, there is no doubt that we shall be advised as to the proper "protective action" to take, long in advance of any such Cataclysm as we have described. As long as we remain loyal "Seekers of the True Light" we need never be frightened by anything that might happen on Earth. In other words, the quality of our thought IS our protection. Good thought, plus good feeling can build strong armour.

Noah, you remember, was warned many years before the Great Flood happened. As a result of his "advance information" Noah was in a position to prepare for what was to come. We should then, cast out all fear or terror from our hearts, and live more and more from "the Spirit"--from the Great God-Presence within us.

While all of us had been relaxing, George was setting up a tape-recorder on a small table in the center of the room. He was now ready to play-back one of the tapes for us to listen to. These contained "messages from outer space" which had been received telepathically by George Van Tassel. It was interesting to learn how this was done. A powerful beam of light was focussed by the Space People (who were in a giant Carrier Ship, positioned on a special "Space Station" 800 miles above the earth) upon George who acted as "receiver". The mind vibrations or "thoughts" of the Space Men were transmitted through this light--which was known as the "Omni-Beam"--in the form of mental images. George then made a "vocal translation" of the ideas he received, and spoke them onto the magnetic tape.

"This first message", he informed us, "was received by us on April 16th, of this year. It is from an individual by the name of Desca. The amazing thing here is that we received this information concerning the harmful effects of the "Polio Vaccine" several weeks before the authorities learned of its danger and withdrew the Vaccine from the general public. Here is the message:

"As most of you know, one of the Ten Commandments states, 'Thou shalt not commit adultery!' In the twisting of words and meanings this has come to be believed in as the violation of marriage laws; human marriage laws of civil origin. This law could have read, 'Thou shalt not commit DILUTION.' The adulteration of anything is the mixing of anything else with it.

"Your propaganda machines there have carried information about the new Polio Vaccine. Whatever it be that is injected into the bloodstream is DILUTION and violation of the commandment, 'Thou shalt not adulterate thyself!'

- 102 -

Flying Saucer Revelations

"The blood is the life of the physical body. Adulteration of the blood changes the frequency, the vibratory rate, and can be the cause of obsession, mental failure, and nerve failure. The blood is the result of a series of chemical-electrical changes in the laboratory of the body. Sudden additions of anything to the bloodstream may, in some cases, bring about a prevention of some particular disease; but the effect of injections of any chemical into the bloodstream will, sooner or later, cause REACTION that will be of a more deadly potential than the original disease could have been. If these Vaccines could be assimilated very gradually over a long period of time the body chemistry could adjust itself to them.

"The new Polio Vaccine (Salk) has not been sufficiently tested for a period of time that would determine conditions that will be apparent in the near future. The ignorance in medicine upon the Earth is in assuming that every individual responds equally to the same application. This will be proven in many ways. The present formula for Polio Vaccine will cause an increase in heart failure, tuberculosis, spinal meningitus, dropsy, and other numerous kidney ailments, and in the long run will bring about an unbalanced mental condition."

Desca's foresight was proven accurate when our Government suddenly clamped down on distribution of the Vaccine in the U. S. Restrictions now, have been made more stringent as regards making of the Vaccine; but nearly a hundred deaths in our nation could be traced to use of the Vaccine at that time.

The next message was extremely fascinating. It was received, George explained, from a planet outside of our Solar System. I shall not try to recall the entire message verbatim. However, the gist of it was that the people on that planet were 400,000 years ahead of us Earthlings in scientific and cultural development.

The geography of their land was flat, whereas our Earth has mountains and hills. All homes and factories on their planet were dome-shaped and made of a translucent material. Machinery, powered by FREE Energy (Magnetic Light-Power) did most of the work, under the watchful eyes of one or two men instead of many men.

Children were educated at home by the parents, who taught by Audio-Visual means, from data issued from a central source. It was considered unnecessary for anyone on that highly evolved planet to use "words" in communicating ideas to each other. Instead, a method of mental telepathy, called "Telethot" was used by the vast majority. For this reason, most of the dwellers of that planet could not speak. As they see it, the mouth was made to eat with, and the brain or rather mind was made to speak with. However, at least one individual in every family was taught to speak in sounds as we do.

After the above mentioned message was heard by our group, George indicated that he expected to have more tape-recorded messages by the next weekend. All who so wished were welcome to return then and hear them.

Nephi and I arose. It was time to be on our way back to the big city. Stepping over to the chair where George was seated, we bid him farewell and thanked him heartily for all his illuminating discourses.

He smiled and shook our hands in a wonderful feeling of love and kinship. We turned and walked up the stone stairs to the door which opened to the desert. Outside, the air was bracing. Pausing briefly, Nephi and I inhaled deeply. This visit to Giant Rock had been a most memorable experience. Much new and vitally important data had been presented to us here. For one thing, our concept of the universe had been expanded tremendously. Now we saw God's universe as a creation of vast and magnificent proportions, with not just two life levels to consider, but a universe with myriads of intelligences of varying levels of life. Suns beyond suns. Planets beyond planets. Solar systems beyond solar systems. Yes, even worlds within worlds...and our Earth but a speck in this mighty universe!

Yet every single electron in an atom is important to the perfect functioning of that atom. Likewise planet Earth is important in the smooth working of the Creator's Master Plan. We are, you and I, in a kindergarten as it were. Our goal is spiritual evolution into a more perfect expression of Life, Love and Light. But we can grow up and out of "kindergarten" if we put our minds to it, just as we grew out of lower grades in school and advanced to the higher grades. If we do this with a conscious will and desire, we'll make much faster progress on the UPWARD PATH leading to the PERFECTED MAN AND WOMAN.

Then, at the proper time, we'll be invited to enjoy a new and thrilling life on a more highly evolved planet than Earth. And, as much as we love Earth, we'll know that our next step upward will be to an even more ideal world than we have known here. We'll realize that ALL WORLDS are essential units in the great design, and each is worthy of our love and our understanding heart.

Yes, this visit with George Van Tassel had filled our minds with many vital new thoughts. The coming gyroscopic SHIFT of the Earth, the amazing concept of FREE Energy, and the idea that some of the inhabitants of other planets possess culture and intelligence that may be millions of years in advance of ours...Nephi and I looked at each other and smiled. Both of us felt raised in consciousness. It could well be that this was only the "beginning" of the many glorious adventures which awaited us with the Space People themselves.

We got into our car and pointed it in the direction of Los Angeles. As we drove away, we knew we would remember Giant Rock!

oooOOOooo

Secrets Of
The Saucer People

by

MICHAEL X

Mystic Monograph No. 3

Flying Saucer Revelations

"SECRETS OF THE SAUCER PEOPLE"

Part One

The Venusian

Several weeks had passed since my eventful trip to Giant Rock (See Mystic Monograph No. 2, "Flying Saucers at Giant Rock") and as yet I had not been privileged to personally contact any of Earth's "Interplanetary Guests".

I was, however, hopeful. When the time was appropriate for me to meet the Saucer People, the meeting would come about in as natural and normal a manner as possible. I knew that it was up to me to take the "first step". How that was to be done I was not at all sure. So I meditated on the problem.

The answer came sooner than I expected. It was so simple as to seem almost childish. Here is the direction I received, as to how I should communicate with the Saucer People:

We live in a mental universe. That is, all space is filled with "mind-stuff" or Ether which can transmit mental vibrations, in the same manner that it transmits radio waves from the Broadcasting Station to your receiving set (radio) at home.

Occultists know that by utilizing the personal energy known as "Vril" it is possible to raise the personal vibrations to an ultra-high frequency or speed. Thought vibrations may then be conveyed on that high frequency to any region in our Solar System.

As most students of esoteric science realize, there are SEVEN ETHERS. Later on, we shall study these Ethers more closely. Four of these Ethers are called, respectively,

    (1)   The Chemical Ether
    (2)   The Life Ether (Prana)
    (3)   The Light Ether
    (4)   The Reflecting Ether

The final three Ethers (5, 6, & 7) are of such a sacred, spiritual nature that only the highest Adepts are permitted to utilize them for mystical and occult purposes. For purposes of contacting the Saucer People, one need only make use of the Light Ether. The reason for this is that they are "Beings of Light" in the fullest sense of the word.

If you wish to listen to a particular radio program on your radio, you must "tune in" to the proper wave-length or frequency. Otherwise you would get a "scramble" of all the various radio programs...that is, you'd pick up portions of different programs as you turned the tuning dial. Only by turning to the right station could you expect to receive the message you desire to hear.

The Saucer People communicate by THINKING ON THE WAVE-LENGTH OF LIGHT. That means we must use the LIGHT ETHER to contact them, as well as to receive messages from them. Ordinary "radio-waves" are transmitted through the Reflecting Ether, NOT the Light Ether. We are concerned only with use of this Light Ether for transmitting THOUGHTS.

So fascinating is this subject of the Seven Ethers, I could write for hours about them and their great importance to us all. That, however, I shall have to leave for another Monograph at some future time. At this point, I believe you would be interested in knowing the details of my unique method of communicating with another world.

On any clear night, look up at the sky and you will quickly see Venus, for it is the brightest star in the sky. Some people call it the "Evening Star"; others refer to it as the "Morning Star", for it is easily visible at both night and morning.

I had long believed that mental communication between planets was not only possible but that it would someday become almost as simple as our "long-distance" phone calls. So I set about the business of attempting to reach the planet Venus by means of Telepathy.

On the night of May 22, 1955, I gazed up at Venus and projected a vibratory "beam of light" from the center of my forehead to the mysterious planet whose influence upon Earth is far greater than humanity can imagine. In the words of the ancient book, "The Commentary", Venus is our Earth's spiritual "prototype". Every sin committed on Earth is felt by Venus", says the Commentary. "She is the Guardian Spirit of the Earth and men. Every change on Venus is felt on and reflected by the Earth.

"Every world has its 'parent star' and 'sister planet'," continues the Commentary. "The Earth is the adopted child and younger brother of Venus, but its inhabitants are of their own kind...all sentient (conscious) complete beings are furnished, in their beginnings, with forms and organisms in full harmony with the nature and states of the sphere they inhabit." It was in line with these ancient teachings that I looked upon Venus as being Earth's teacher.

I was, during this attempt at "space telepathy", comfortably positioned on the roof of my house. There I was least liable to disturbance while concentrating. Also, it was quiet and dark so that I had no difficulty in focussing my thoughts. The message I decided to "transmit" to Venus was this:

"MICHAEL OF EARTH CALLING VENUS. COME IN VENUS. COME IN VENUS. OVER."

Flying Saucer Revelations

This is the established "form" of communication language used by all Airline pilots on Earth. It is standard radio practice. I was, of course, not at all sure that interplanetary beings referred to their own planet as "Venus" or to ours as "Earth". There would be, however, a mutual "meeting of the minds" as to what I meant. This I was sure of, since I would "transmit" in the form of Mind Images and Pictures rather than words.

It was 10:00 P.M. For nearly one half-hour I concentrated on sending my message. I would transmit my thought for 5 minutes, then wait receptively for 5 minutes. There was no response. At about 10:30 P.M. I gave the whole thing up for the night and dozed off to sleep on a cot which I had hauled up to the rooftop for this special purpose.

At 2:00 A.M. an amazing thing happened. A voice was calling my name. "MICHAEL, MICHAEL..." It kept saying, in penetrating, melodious tones. It was an extremely beautiful voice, clear and bell-like. Instinctively, I opened my eyes. No other human being was in sight. I was entirely alone on my cot in the darkness and only the stars and the shimmering moon were visible.

A vivid dream, I thought to myself as I closed my eyes to resume sleeping. Then I knew this was not a dream but a reality. A voice was speaking to me slowly and distinctly, repeating my name. I responded by means of Mental Telepathy as best I could.

"Who are you?" was all I could think to say, for I still thought it possible that my mind might be "playing tricks" on me.

"I am a human being, much like yourself." The voice replied, after what seemed like a delay of nearly a full minute. "My planet is the one you call 'Venus'. We have intercepted your communication by Telethot, and are pleased to make this contact with you."

The voice of the Venusian continued: "We have known of your work along the lines of Occult Science," he said, "and consider it good. You and your companions are moving in the right direction. It is our purpose to guide you, from time to time, without superimposing our will upon yours. I am not at liberty to reveal certain details in regard to this planet; but questions of a general nature can be answered freely by us."

"Tell me something of your science and culture." I inquired, "Also, what is your means of power for interplanetary flight?"

"We are nearing the middle of our 7th Planetary Round", replied the Venusian. "You people of Terra (Earth) are in the midst of your 4th Round. In simple terms, this means we are nearly fifteen million years ahead of your planet in respect to global evolution. As you know, every planet begins its life in an etheric condition. Gradually, after several millions of years, it evolves into a sphere of physical matter that is hard and condensed. Still later, when the planet reaches its final Round, there is a reversal of the trend. It returns again to its original state of soft, etheric matter.

"Consider a baby on your Earth;" said the Venusian, "At birth the baby's body and bone structure are extremely soft, pliable and almost 'fluid' in consistency. As the body matures, the bones harden and become more brittle. The entire form becomes tougher and appears more solid and lasting.

"Planets too, are bodies. They are also 'beings' on their own life level, having an evolutionary path of their own to follow.

"It is almost beyond the comprehension of Earth beings to grasp the tremendous Knowledge that our people of 'Venus' have attained down through the milleniums of Time.

"Perhaps the first fact you should become aware of, insofar as we Venusians are concerned, is that all of our people have long ago discovered their correct relationship with the 'Father' of the Cosmic Universe in which we are living. We know and use as a working principle, the immense power of the Creator's Will which is expressed through the action of physical light in all Galactic Universes."

There was a long pause. Apparently the speaker desired his last thought to "sink in" for it was five minutes before his next idea came spinning across the thousands of miles between himself and me.

The next thing he said was, "Michael, am I clear? Are you getting tired?"

I immediately replied that I was not tired and that I was receiving his thought clearly, and would he please continue?

"The 'will' of the Creator is eternally active in all his creations," explained my Venusian teacher. "His 'will' works through Man, by means of the 'light' whithin that 'lighteth every man that cometh into the world'. This is the positive or spiritual power in Conscious Man and Woman.

"The Mystic purpose of all created human intelligences is to actively express love, which is the stabilizing power that harmonizes the impelling power of 'will'. This brings about a balance---and is the primary law of the entire Cosmos."

As he said these things, I found myself unconsciously 'linking' them up with one of Christ's mysterious expressions, "The Father works, and I work". Everything in the Cosmos was seeking fulfillment --balance--rest.

"What you call 'motion' is the natural result of a universal need in all material things, to achieve a condition of balance. It is through 'voiding' certain opposing forces, that all things are able to move. When the resisting energies have been fully 'voided', motion then ceases automatically."

To the Venusian, the ideas he was presenting were "elementary" but to my mind they seemed at least slightly "bewildering". He had an entirely different way of thinking and as yet I was not prepared for it. His mind thought in terms of PRIMARY CAUSES, all based on Cosmic laws, which are entirely TRUE in essence. We of Earth, for the most part, are not centered in true cause, but are "off-centered" in EFFECTS. In other words, we know HOW many things happen, but we haven't the slightest idea WHY they happen.

For several days prior to my "telephone" contact with a being from another world, I had been making up a "list" of questions to ask such a being. As you of course realize, certain questions which deal with matters beyond our immediate scope of interest, or which are considered "restricted" by the Space People, were not included in the list.

However, I did include a great variety of questions. Most of them are direct and simple. Some were complex and deep. When the Venusian mind-waves reached mine, these are some of the questions I asked and the answers I was given by my instructor:

QUESTION: "What do your people (The Venusians) look like?

ANSWER: "Venusians are of two sexes, male and female, as on your planet. Many of our Adepts are androgynous, having both masculine and feminine polarities perfectly balanced in the physical body. Our facial features are somewhat different, being smoother and broader, especially the forehead. Centuries of mental telepathy have produced our characteristics in this respect."

QUESTION: "Physically, then, you resemble to a considerable extent, a 'humanoid'?"

ANSWER: "Yes. Our average height is 5'-7". However, there is a difference in bodily weight and structure as compared with Earthlings. If you should come to our planet you would weigh slightly more than you do on Earth, to compensate for the fact that our planet is only 80% as large in mass as your Earth. Our bodies are more etheric, in keeping with the evolutionary stage of our planet and are therefore lighter in weight than yours. The atomic structure is less dense and the radiation of the 'light within' is greater, ennabling us to appear young and beautiful at a much greater age than you of Earth are yet able to appear. The humanoid form is found on almost every habitable planet in space. The big difference between planets is largely in the mental and spiritual development achieved."

* * * * *

Flying Saucer Revelations

Flying Saucer Revelations

"SECRETS OF THE SAUCER PEOPLE"

Part Two

Secrets of The Universe

QUESTION: "Do the 'visitors' from outer space all come from your planet Venus?"

ANSWER: "Most of the Space People who have landed on Earth do come from Venus; many are from Mars. A great many extra-terrestial visitors also have come from other densities in the Cosmos. Some have even come from other Solar systems than ours. They were on exploratory flights."

Q: "Is interplanetary flight as dangerous and difficult as it appears to be?"

A: "This depends. If you try to conquer space with 'rocket-power' or 'atomic engines' it would be utterly disastrous. A space flight powered by FREE Energy would be an entirely different matter. You would be sure of getting to your destination because you could depend on never running out of fuel since it is available in all parts of this Solar System. More important, by using FREE Energy, you would be able to get back to the original point of departure. Space People have been flying between planets for thousands and thousands of years. To us it is essentially a simple matter, and it is extremely rare that any of our ships are lost through space accidents.

Q: "Such accidents do occur?"

A: "Yes, though infrequently. As long as our space navigators stay within the vortex of this particular Solar System, little danger exists. It is when flights are made between separate universes that miscalculations may be made."

Q: What do you mean by 'vortex'?"

A: "A vortex is an energy field which has the shape of a whirlpool or spiral. In our universe, the Sun radiates the 'Master Vortex'. This produces lines of magnetic force extending to the outermost ends of this Solar System. Within the Master Vortex is the sub-vortex of Mercury, Venus, Earth, Mars, Jupiter, Saturn, and so on. All of these small vortices within the Sun's vortex are known as the 'Great Serpent', or the 'Solar Phalanx'. Space navigators as a rule stay inside of the Solar Phalanx."

Q: "How do Flying Saucers fly?"

A: "I assume you mean our Space Discs. We also call them 'Fire-Ships", because of their glowing, fiery appearance in operation. The means of propulsion is simple enough to understand IF you first grasp the principle of the 'Master Vortex'. A space Disc moves through space by generating a small vortex of its own, within the ship. This vortex of energy is a miniature 'force field'. It is produced and sustained by the great vortex of the Sun itself. When we extend this force field outside of the Space Disc, its lines of magnetic force cut across the primary lines of the Sun's Master Vortex. The effect of this is brilliant, glowing light. Also, the Space Disc instantly goes into motion, following the lines of the Great Vortex. It is trying to 'void' itself by moving from the negative phase of the Vortex to the positive."

Q: "How can the Saucer People remain alive inside a Space Disc, if the Disc becomes a glowing, fiery light?"

A: "There is an opposite polarity between the outside of the Disc and the inside. This creates the effect of hot light on the outer surface or 'skin', and gives a reverse effect of 'cold light' on the inside surface. To simplify this in your mind, you need to know that force always moves--not in straight lines--but in circles, so that it always returns to itself. Within our Spacecraft, cold is opposing heat so we remain cool instead of being as you say, 'cremated'."

B: "What does the surface of Venus look like? Is it hot, 'sand-blasted--that planet that our astronomers think it is?"

A: "No. The scientists of Earth are quite mistaken about that. Venus is extremely verdant and luxuriant with vegetation. It has, however, a predominant blue color whereas on Earth the leaf color is green. Our atmosphere is heavier than that of Earth, so we are protected from excessive sunlight. Because your scientists could not see through our atmosphere, they assumed the worst."

Q: "What causes the rotation of the planets?"

A: "Each planet is surrounded by its own smaller 'Sub-Vortex' or force-field. This field is operative within the larger field of the Sun. As a result, it intercepts the lines of force of the Master Vortex--causing the planet to manifest MOTION in an effort to escape from an unbalanced energy condition. So the sphere rotates."

Q: "Is that a form of perpetual motion, or FREE Energy?"

A: "Yes, it is FREE Energy, or the power that runs the universe we live in."

Q: "Is there a simple key to use in order to understand HOW this FREE Energy works?"

A: "The secret lies simply in gaining a basic 'working knowledge' of Vortexya---that is, the principles of Vortices."

Q: "Do the Venusian people utilize FREE Energy in other ways, besides propelling their Spacecraft by means of it?"

A: "Yes, nearly all the advanced intelligences of the space worlds make use of the universal power of Vortexya in countless practical ways. We use Free Energy to run our factories, light our dwellings, propel our vehicles, and perform a million other necessary services for us. For instance, in our homes it produces light without the need for any containing globes whatsoever."

Q: "Will you explain the method? As you know, we on Earth use light bulbs which have the air extracted from them so that a wire filament can burn or glow within the vacuum, thus producing electric light. Do you have a simpler method of creating light?"

A: "Indeed we have. There is no need for 'wires' or 'bulbs' or vacuum conditions when you cross magnetic lines of force at right angles. That produces the same kind of light as the 'daylight' of nature. It is the Light Ether manifesting itself visibly. We Venusians use this natural form of light in all of our buildings, which, incidentally, are semi-spherical inshape, and formed of a hard, translucent type of plastic."

Q: "Can you tell me why your Space People are coming to this Earth, and what they desire of me and my fellow beings?"

A: "We come to guide Mankind on Earth into the more harmonious, spiritual life. Our purpose is to show Earthlings the secret of all evolution into a higher, grander form of expression and awareness. We are here to inspire Man to a complete dedication of self to the purposes of the Creator. This is in truth the Great Work to which many are called but few are chosen. Your mind is God's mind, whether you realize it or not; for there is but one Mind in the Cosmos. When you consciously know that, you begin to serve the higher Ideals which your spirit knows."

Q: "What is God's 'will' for Man?"

A: "More Life, Love, Truth, and Beauty."

Q: "Does the universe have a lesson to teach Mankind? As you know, we humans are often fearful, anxious and despondent."

A: "Yes. The universe teaches us to seek the 'centre' of peace and harmony within is, and regulate our lives from this one centre. That is how the life of the entire universe with all its planets and suns and stars is regulated. What beauty resides at the centre of things --what order--system! While the great machinery of life goes on throughout the vast Macrocosm, here at the starting-point of all is peace. Here unending harmony abides, a repose which no calamity can disturb. Worlds may end, terrible disasters may happen, wars may be fought and earthquakes shake the face of planets. But still the universe MOVES FORWARD. The pulse of life never stops, the centre remains unhurt. Man needs this calm SERENITY."

Q: "Do you suffer from Diseases of any kind of Venus, or during space flights?

A: "Our people have long since learned the 'inner' causes of disease, and are aware that destructive thoughts or negative emotions (fear, hatred, jealousy, resentment, revenge, etc.) cause an unbalanced physical condition. Why? Because they cause a state of 'contraction' in all of the bodily cells. On the other hand constructive and harmonious thoughts produce E-X-P-A-N-S-I-O-N in all the cells. We realize that contraction is death and expansion is life. So we choose to expand into continually greater L I F E.

"Space flights no longer cause us any physical difficulty. This is because our Spacecraft produces its own 'synthetic gravity' during flight, and also produces its own air of the proper warmth and density.

"The external cold of outer space cannot hurt us, since we utilize the principles of Navaz or Night-Side forces to maintain healthful and comfortable living conditions inside our Spacecraft."

Q: "What do you mean by 'Navaz'?"

A: "That is our term for the Night-Side of Nature. This refers to the circular progression of the forces of the Vortex from the Sun. The lines of force follow a circular path out from the Sun and then return again. Moving from the Sun they belong to the 'Light-Side' of Nature; but when moving back to the Sun they belong to Navaz or the 'Night-Side'."

"Scientists on Earth know practically nothing of the forces found in the Night-Side of Nature. When they do discover these subtle forces, they will have the secret of 'repulsion by levitation'... as well as other secrets Man on Earth has not even imagined. Neither Earth, air, the depth of the seas nor those of interstellar space will hold secrets from that man who approaches from the Godward side to gain knowledge of Navaz."

Q: "Do you require any special kind of food to sustain you on long flights from one planet to another?"

A: "For space travel purposes, we take along with us a concentrated type of food resembling a round, flat wafer. On Venus, these wafers have been subjected to a mind-wave process we call 'Thought-conditioning'. The effect of this is to give the wafer whatever special food taste we desire to enjoy. For example, if we are hungry for a certain 'favorite' food we merely think of that and the wafer will taste like that food. An Earthling, for instance, might think of 'roast beef' or 'fried chicken' and upon eating the wafers would experience precisely the 'taste' reaction in his sensory nerves that he would if he were enjoying the real thing."

Q: "What effects are resulting in the universe from the series of atomic blasts we have been setting off on Earth?"

Flying Saucer Revelations

A: "Atomic nuclear explosions on your planet Earth are a most serious matter. Far more so than your scientists realize. Each explosion disrupts the etheric levels of life such as Atmospherea and Etherea. (See Monograph #4, "The Magic of Ether Ships") That is another reason why Space Ships are landing on Earth in constantly greater numbers. We seek to prevent this kind of destructiveness."

Q: "How do you accomplish your mental and scientific 'miracles'? I have heard the Space People have learned to forestall physical death for centuries. Could you give me and my friends some 'hint' as to your advanced techniques?"

A: "Yes, I can. We have attained mastery of the universal forces unknown to your Earth scientists. Indeed, they can never hope to discover these subtle powers because they are approaching them from the side of the 'physical eye' instead of from the side of the 'spiritual eye'. In the realm beyond magnetism are yet other forces, superior and more intense in vibratory frequency. These forces are operatid BY THE MIND. Mind is of the Creator, and is the sustaining, creating source of everything that exists. An Adept learns how to raise personal vibration up to the higher levels of 'Odic' or Mind-Force. This has sometimes been referred to as 'Vril' and is a wonderful power to acquire. By its use we can almost instantly re-create the cells of the physical body...all this being done by the conscious direction of THOUGHT. With 'Vril' a human being is enabled to retain his or her physical body for a life span of from 300 to 1500 years."

As the Venusian's reply reached me, I suddenly noticed a feeling of complete weariness which seemed to overpower me. This was due, no doubt, to the length of time we had been in 'communication' by Telethot.

Sadly I brought our conversation to an end, after being assured by him that there would be further 'conversations' in the near future. "There is more to talk about," the Space Master said, "and more to learn." A few parting instructions were given to me then, as to how and when the next telethot communication should take place. Then the conversation broke off and I fell into a deep sleep that lasted for many hours.

For days after the communication I felt glorious. That sense of "living" in a great universe of light--electro-magnetic waves of light, wherein 'all things are possible'--became constantly more real to me. I thought of you, dear friend, who would read of that experience in the pages of this Monograph. And I saw you...moving ever Onward, Upward, and Godward...to the highest Realms of Mystic Light with the "Elect" of Mankind.

oooOOOooo

Flying Saucer Revelations

The Magic
Of Ether Ships

by

MICHAEL X

Mystic Monograph No. 4

Flying Saucer Revelations

Flying Saucer Revelations

"THE MAGIC OF ETHER SHIPS"

Part One

The Etheric Worlds

Suppose--just for a moment--that you had "passed out of the physical embodiment" and are now "dead". No...don't shudder at the
thought of physical death. You, as a good student of the deeper mysteries of life, need't have the slightest feeling of fear or anxiety
in regard to your "transition". Knowledge and love enable us to cast
out even the age-old inherited fear of experiencing so-called "death".
So we intend to continually gain a more complete picture of that human
episode known as death. The more we learn of the subtle or "occult"
side of things, the less use we have for fear.

Going back to our original idea, that quite suddenly you "gave
up the ghost" and died...what do you think you would see? That is,
what would your spirit--the immortal part of you--what would it see
on the "other side" of Life's mystic curtain? If your mind is somewhat dim on that question, be of good cheer and read on, for it IS a
mighty big question, and one that has been baffling mortal man for
centuries.

In the pages you are now reading, some fascinating new data will
be presented to you, which we trust will throw some needed light on
this subject of human "life levels". Most of this new information
has been given to us by the Space People, through various contacts
with humans on Earth. Some of these contacts have been made in recent
times by such individuals as George Adamski, George Van Tassel,
Truman Bethurum, Orfeo Angelucci and many others too numerous to
mention.

To each of these Earthlings has been given information of a
dimensionally greater universe than any of us have been aware of
before. Now, however, with this new data that has come to us from
the Space People, we are getting answers to vital questions.

In 1882, long before the people of our planet had even heard of
"Flying Saucers", a man by the name of John Ballou Newbrough received
a psychic communication from one of the Space People. This intelligent Being from another world, told John Newbrough that he must
write a book by "remote control". That is, the Space Master would
dictate the book, and John would transcribe it onto paper, after
receiving the message.

Back in those early days, the typewriter had just been invented
and was quite a crude affair in comparison to 1955 models. Never-
the less, the Space Master instructed John to purchase a typewriter
and to merely hold his hands over the keys each morning an hour before dawn. John did so and found to his utter amazement that his

hands typed out the thoughts of the Space Master automatically, without his conscious control. He was told, incidentally, that he was NOT to read what he was writing until the manuscript was completed.

At the end of one year, the immense project had been completed ...all 891 pages of it. And he was instructed to publish it under the title of "OAHSPE", a New Bible. This book was not, mind you, intended to make our Christian Bible "obsolete" in any respect. Rather it was intended to supplement all the former Bibles, Vedas and other sacred books...and to show how all the former bibles are all parts of one stupendous plan of our Heavenly Creator for bringing light to earthly mortals, even as you and I.

The big thing we are interested in at this moment is the unique fact that OAHSPE was written by means of "Telethot" communication between an Earthling and a wise being from another time-space dimension. So when we read OAHSPE we know how it feels to view life, the creation on Earth, the higher spiritual worlds, etc., THROUGH THE EYES OF ONE OF THE SPACE PEOPLE!

Please do not misunderstand me. I am not trying to "sell" the book OAHSPE, for that is not my publication. My object is simply to call your attention to OAHSPE insofar as it relates to Flying Discs and our greater knowledge of the "Other Worlds".

Most public libraries have a copy of OAHSPE that you can secure in case you are interested in further "research" into its revelations. Or, it can be obtained by writing to The Essenes of Kosmon, Rt. 2, Box 26-A, Montrose, Colorado. Such books as OAHSPE (Meaning Sky, Earth and Spirit) are given mankind but once each 3,000 years. It gives light on Man's origin, purpose and destiny; the history of the planet, of the human races, of every major religion. Price of the book is $5.00 postpaid.

In regard to these "Other Worlds" we mentioned a moment ago, we refer to the Etheric Worlds. Sometimes these are called "planes". They are actual worlds of finer physical matter known as "etheric matter". Though you and I cannot see these etheric worlds with the normal physical eye, they CAN be seen by our "inner" or spiritual eye.

There are just TWO Etheric worlds. They are spherical in shape just as our Earth is. And they interpenetrate and surround the Earth. Of course, the average "man in the street" hasn't the slightest inkling of the fact that these two invisible worlds are passing right through him at all times.

It is only when that person "dies" that his spiritual eye wakes up and sees those Etheric Realms. Quite naturally, he is, to say the least, startled by the sight. It is all so completely "strange" to him that he is totally unprepared to function like a good "spirit" should. The Space People tell us that countless millions of souls remain on the lower levels of the spirit-world for hundreds of years.

Flying Saucer Revelations

They have never learned of the existence of the HIGHER HEAVEN WORLDS and so they make no effort to go up higher.

This is deplorable. However, it is not in the least necessary for a human soul to tolerate undue hardship on any level of life. You can, for example, raise your own living standard simply by positive thinking and a determined will. There will always be those who "gravitate" to the "flop-house" environment simply because they think "in reverse".

There are, then, actually THREE WORLDS IN ONE. The physical Earth, and the other two, "intermeshing" Etheric worlds. These last two worlds are known as "Atmospherea" and "Etherea". If you will please note the diagram on the front page of this Monograph you will gain a clearer picture of these invisible worlds. Notice that Atmospherea extends upward from the Earth's surface, and into the high stratosphere several miles above the Earth.

Atmospherea consists of much denser "etheric matter" than is found in Etherea. That is why Atmospherea is the first Density you and I and all mortals will "visit" when and IF we should happen to pass out of physical embodiment. However, since there are certain methods and practices we can follow to keep our physical bodies in vital "balance" at all times, there is absolutely no need to "shuffle off this mortal coil" by dying. As you may recall, few of the true ADEPTS of history ever gave up their physical body.

Instead, they perfected the physical by refining the atomic structures of the cells. Enoch, you will remember, did not go through the experience of death. He "walked with God" and was taken up by the Space People to another planet where he was needed. I am firmly convinced that you and I can and will realize the same privilege in due time.

Human beings of the "mass-minded" category, naturally wake up in the next Density when they die. They then only possess the finer Etheric or Astral body, having moved out of the denser physical body --and "lost it" because of having broken the "Silver Cord". They are then known as "spirits". But here is the important thing to realize: The mere fact that a person becomes a "spirit" does not necessarily make him or her a "superbeing" all at once. Not at all. A "spirit" or "departed one" still remains much the same as he did before his transition. That is, he has the same mental attitude that he had on Earth. However, due to the fact that the molecules that make up the Etheric worlds obey laws different from those governing matter on Earth, a "spirit" has to study those laws and then learn how to apply them properly.

It is only through mastering all the natural laws that govern Atmospherea, that a spirit being, or "departed one" is able to progress to the next higher density. That is to Etherea, or the Third Density of etheric matter.

Flying Saucer Revelations

The Ethereans dwell in etheric regions which extend above and beyond Atmospherea. They possess much finer etheric bodies than do the Atmosphereans. Etherean angels are beautiful, glorified beings. They are often called "Celestials". Mentally, they express an extremely high order of intelligence. In fact, so intelligent are they that they are allowed to govern certain stars, planets and worlds. But here is the interesting point:

As stated previously, all etheric beings still function in bodies made of physical matter. True, it is much finer than material we see on earth. Nevertheless, angels must retain bodies of extremely fine matter until the time comes for them to make their next "upward" spiritual step.

In the meantime, while they are learning important lessons of life in Etherea, the people of that world make use of "Fire-Ships" or Space Discs, to fly on important missions. These vehicles (also called "Ether Ships") are built by the Spacecraft Constructors of Etherea and Atmospherea, to carry the inhabitants from place to place. In this manner the angels of the lower and higher heavens learn the secrets of the Universe.

There is much magic connected with the Ether Ships and their operation. That is, it appears to be "magic" to us Earthlings, for we do not as yet comprehend it fully. It is only magical to us until we can gain greater knowledge of the HOW and the WHY of it.

In the book OAHSPE you will find many enlightening descriptions of Ether Ships. As most students of Saucer Phenomena are aware, the motive power for some of these discs is produced by musical sound activated by the action of the pilot's will-power.

For instance, on page 209 in the section relating to Fragapatti, Son of Jehovih, Chapter XIII, Paragraph 4, we read:

"Now struck up the Ethereans with music, thirty thousand of them, but soft and gentle as a breath of wind, carrying the tones around about the SHIP, even as an endless echo, calling and answering from all possible directions, a continuous and enrapturing change, as if near, and as if far off. So that the uninformed knew not whence the music came nor how it was produced.

"All these things were set to working order just as the great Avalanza (Ether Ship) was ready to start. Then Fragapatti went into the ship, being almost the last one to enter. Already the light was gathering bright and dense about him, his head almost hid in the brilliancy of the halo. And then he called out:

"Arise! Arise! In Jehovih's name, upward rise! And as he spake, behold the avalanza MOVED WITH HIS WILL, for all the hosts (student angels) joined in the same expression, and presently started upward the great Fire-Ship; leaving the burning walls and signal centres flickering below, so that even hell overthrown shone with great grandeur."

Flying Saucer Revelations

Again, on page 317, from the section relating to Cpenta-Armij, Daughter of Jehovih, Paragraph 19, we find:

"By music alone, some their ships propelled, the vibratory chords affording power sufficient in such high-skilled hands, and the tunes changing according to the regions traversed. Others, even by colors made in the waves of sound, went forward, carrying millions of angels, every one attuned so perfectly that his very presence lent power and beauty to that monarch vessel."

We should realize that, just as there are a great variety of different makes and models of automobiles and airplanes here on Earth, likewise, there exist a million varieties of Spacecraft (including Ether Ships). Some are in the shape of silvery discs. Some are cigar shaped. Some resemble bells, with a super-structure (see George Adamski's book, "Flying Saucers Have Landed"). Still others may have strange forms as yet unknown to us. However, Ether Ships have power to become visible and invisible. They can appear and disappear. Spacecraft from other denser physical planets remain visible to the eye. That is, they are visible when moving at slow speeds, or when hovering, or when they have landed.

Of course, it is obvious that any interplanetary craft, regardless of whether it is of physical or etheric construction, becomes increasingly less visible the faster it travels. After a Flying Saucer, for example, has reached maximum acceleration it is moving at the speed of 186,000 miles per second. This is the rate of speed attained by light, so the effect produced by a material object that attains that velocity would be something like a streak of light.

In future Mystic Monographs, we shall have more to say about the higher "life levels"--Atmospherea and Etherea--which will open up many new doors of understanding to you. You will be taught how to make certain of your "graduation" from Atmospherea (the next Density) in the briefest time possible, so that you can move up and away from the 2nd Density and into the 3rd Density of Etherea.

I am sure you will agree that it is foolish for any intelligent being to settle for anything less than the best in life. As an instance of this, why be satisfied with HALF-WAY answers to the many important questions you have about life and about yourself? Why not dig a little beneath the "surface" of things and find out some of the REAL REASONS for the seemingly "mysterious" happenings that go on?

All things can be explained...in a way that satisfies both the mind and the soul. Every effect has a CAUSE. You are learning some of the really important causes right now. You are getting acquainted with a much larger universe now; and you can see that you will have many exciting and thrilling NEW lessons to master when you yourself are one day ready to take your place in the higher Heaven Worlds.

Flying Saucer Revelations

Flying Saucer Revelations

"THE MAGIC OF ETHER SHIPS"

Part Two

The Great Harvest

Our planet Earth is on a mystical journey through space. That is what our scientists mean when they say that we live in an "expanding universe". Our Solar System with all its planets, moons and stars, is moving constantly upward and outward into higher regions of cosmic space.

One of these regions is known by the name of "Dan" which means "Light". In this region are found some of the higher Etherean kingdoms. Therefore, our Earth must move through the regions of Dan, as it spirals onward and ever outward in space and time.

We are entering the Regions of Dan now. Consequently, you and I are living in the "Time of Dan", and so are receiving higher spiritual vibrations from this Region as our Earth rotates through it.

Quite naturally, the influence of this higher Etheric Realm upon mortals on Earth is considerable. That is why more and more men and women in all walks of life, and of all ages, are "looking to the sky" and to the Space People, for spiritual wisdom. Many people are puzzled over the things that are "coming upon the earth". They do not have even a slight "inkling" of what is in store for our world and its inhabitants.

As you well know, the subject of "Flying Saucers" is no longer something to be ridiculed or "laughed away". So many people have seen the Discs that mankind is finally waking up to the fact that "there are more things in heaven and earth....than are dreamed of in our philosophies" as Shakespeare said. We are beginning to accept Flying Discs and Spacemen as a reality to be considered. That is good. Of course, students of the mystic and occult side of nature have known about Flying Discs and similar phenomena for hundreds and thousands of years. We have long recognized "Saucers" for what they are: portents of THE COMING SPIRITUAL AGE!

A most illuminating occult explanation of Ether Ships and their mystic purpose, is revealed to us in the Book of Jehovih, from OAHSPE. Paragraph 13 tells us:

"And God shall appoint Chiefs under him who shall go down and dwell on the Earth with mortals; and such Chiefs" labor shall be with mortals for their RESURRECTION. And these Chiefs shall be called Lords, for they are Gods of Land, which is the lowest rank of My commissioned Gods.

"And God and his Lords shall have dominion from 200 years to 1000 or more years; but never more than 3000 years. (Length of Minor Cycle). According to the regions of Dan (Light) into which I bring the Earth, so shall be the terms of the office of My Gods and My Lords.

"And God and His Lords shall raise up officers to be their successors; by Him and by them shall they be appointed and crowned in My Name.

"At the termination of the dominion of My God and His Lords shall gather together in these My bound heavens, all such angels as have been prepared in wisdom and strength for resurrection to My Etherean Kingdoms. And these angels shall be called Brides and Bridegrooms to Jehovih, for they are Mine and in My service.

"And to God and his Lords, with the Brides and Bridegrooms, will I send down from Etherea SHIPS (Ether Ships) in the time of Dan; by My Etherean Gods and Goddesses shall the ships descend to these heavens, and receive God and His Lords with the Brides and Bridegrooms, and carry them up to the exalted regions I have prepared for them.

"And all such as ascend shall be called a Harvest unto Me through My God and Lords."

The "Chiefs" who come down to the Earth and dwell with mortals, are the Space People who are still "in the Flesh". That is, they are not returning from the dead for they never died. By occult knowledge they continued living on in the same bodies as of this earth. In other words, the "Chiefs" have conquered that last enemy called "Death".

Their purpose is to teach all mortals who have proven themselves worthy of such knowledge, that they too can conquer Death. However, immortality of the physical body will only be realized by progressive individuals who are capable of attaining it. We must remember that 'many are called, but few are chosen". This applies here also.

As you have already noted, millions of human beings now living on Earth will NOT survive the next 45 years physically. They will-- due to one cause of another--pass out of physical embodiment before the next era of Peace and Plenty (The Millenium) arrives. Among these millions of souls will be many wonderful people, men and women who are highly evolved individuals. The mere fact that they had to pass through the experience called Death does not mean that they are inferior beings. Actually, many of them will be the "cream of the crop" of mortals. They simply neglected to study the important science of "Immortality" during Earth Life.

What then, will happen to these people? According to the book of Jehovih, they will, after death, find themselves dwelling in the heavens of Atmospherea, the next Density beyond the material Earth. There they will remain until the "Time of Dan", which occurs frequently (once every several hundred years). Then, the "Great Harvest" of Angels takes place in the heaven worlds.

Flying Saucer Revelations

The Ethereans descend in their Ether Ships to "Harvest" the "Elect" or good souls in Atmospherea. Then the Ethereans ascend with several million new angels which have been "emancipated" from Atmospherea (the lower heavens) and enter into the higher heavens of Etherea...the Celestial Realm.

As we mentioned previously, our planet is moving into the higher etheric regions at this very moment, and has been doing so for the past ten years. Consequently, the "Great Harvest" is on right now in the Etheric kingdoms. The Ethereans are intensely active in the "Second Density" (Atmospherea) collecting into their Fire-Ships all those who are prepared for the great new journey which is onward, upward and Godward into the Third Density or Etherea.

Why use Ether Ships for this purpose? Why do spirits or angels require anything as cumbersome as a "Space Ship" in order to go from one place to another in the etheric realms? Why not just fly with their spirit body and soar up into the higher kingdoms?

The answer is, the astral bodies of the people living in Atmospherea, the lower heaven world, are much too densified to be able to function comfortably in Etherea. You might liken this situation to deep sea diving. If we send a diver down into the extreme depths of the ocean, we have to protect his body by encasing it in a special diving suit built to withstand the pressure below. Now, once our diver reaches the levels of the ocean, we must NOT bring him up to the surface of the water suddenly or he will suffer extreme pain. He may even develop a condition known as the "bends", if he is moved too rapidly from high pressure to low pressure. Again, fishes of the deep-sea variety are known to burst when brought up into the upper levels of the ocean water.

The environmental differences between Density 1 (material earth) Density 2 (Atmospherea) and Density 3 (Etherea) are so pronounced, some means of protection must be afforded to bodies of those who attempt to oove freely through those densities.

Ether Ships are the logical solution to this problem of transportation between the 2nd Density and Etherea. In the first place, Ether Ships are not cumbersome or unwieldy as would be, for example, our jet planes or six motored transport planes or even our helpful helicopters. Instead, Ether Ships are sleek, smooth, luxurious vessels which glide through space serenely and peacefully.

In the second place, although those persons who experienced "death" on earth, and who are now living in Atmospherea, are able to "fly" with ease through the Atmosphere of that Density (including our own material density of earth), they cannot fly beyond the uppermost spacial regions of Atmospherea. To do so would cause them much pain. I am speaking now of flights in the etheric or "astral" body only, without the use of Spacecraft of any kind. So you see that even those individuals living in the next Density (atmospherea) are limited the same as you and I, though not to the same extent. The point is, they do have their limitations, and must observe them.

Human beings, that is, Earthlings, who have developed their spiritual sight through certain occult practices, are able to clair-voyantly SEE the Ether Ships as they descend into Atmospherea for the "Great Harvest". As you now realize, this is happening more and more frequently as we move into the higher etheric regions of light.

Many persons assert they have seen Ether Ships which seemed to appear and disappear at will. I have been asked many times for my opinion as to how such phenomena occurs. My reply has always been, that since the Ethereans are more highly evolved beings mentally and spiritually than we are at this time, it is no great trick for them to "materialize" and "dematerialize" their spacecraft. All that is required for an etherean ship to suddenly become visible to us, is a change in the "molecular polarity" of the ship. This could be done by mind force or by electronic means. The ship would then "attract" denser physical matter to it, causing it to "appear".

On the other hand, by reversing this particular polarity, the ship again returns to its original condition of "invisibility" because it is made of finer-etheric matter than we are accustomed to seeing physically.

Summing up what we have been talking about in the last two or three pages, there are several general conclusions we can arrive at in regard to the "Ether Ships".

1.   They are designed to transport the good souls from Atmos-pherea into Etherea. This being accomplished once every several hundred years. It is the "Great Harvest".

2.   They are specially "pressurized" spacecraft of finer etheric density than other spacecraft from material densities. As the chosen Atmospherean angels (the host) are transported upward into higher regions of etherean space, they are assisted by the Ethereans to "raise their vibrations" so they will be able to dwell comfortably in Etherea.

3.   Without Ether Ships millions of souls dwelling in Atmospherea would never be able to leave the 2nd Density and progress higher into the 3rd Density of Etherea.

4.   They (Ether Ships) have the power to become visible or in-visible to our eyes. A good illustration of this power is given in OAHSPE, book of Sethantes, page 24, paragraphs 8 & 9. I quote:

"When the ship of the hosts of God came to the city of Uldoo, mortals SAW it high up in the air, and they feared and ran hastily to consult the prophet of the Lord. And the prophet said: Behold, God appeareth in a sea of fire (glowing ether ship) in the firmament of Heaven.

"And God caused the Ship to be made unseen, that fear might subside on earth, and he descended with his hosts into the house of the Lord, and they went and touched the things mortals had builded that they might perceive corporeally."

5. Ether Ships are NOT the same craft that come from Venus, Mars, and other dense worlds much like our own planet. Instead, they come from another dimension entirely...namely, the 4-dimensional Space-Time world of Etherea, which is one of the etheric or invisible worlds interpenetrating Earth.

Due to the fact that the Ethereans are beings of a higher dimensional world, they may not look very much like us Earth Folk when they are functioning in their natural "habitat". However, when they come into a denser plane to carry out some good mission, they use bodies just like we do. Of course, they might be a little taller or shorter possibly—but much more attractive and with a much greater spiritual understanding than we have.

At the present time the general public is largely "in the dark" regarding the Ether Ship mystery. Most people have heard, read about or actually seen "Flying Saucers"—which are NOT Ether Ships, as we have learned in this study. However, few persons have discovered the story of these INTERDIMENSIONAL CRAFT that originate in Etheric Realms!

Quite true, the newspapers, the radio, and television reporters are "playing down" the whole astounding episode. There is an enforced "hush-hush" rule among the newscasters. The idea is to treat "Flying Saucers" and Spacemen" as one big joke, and then let it go at that. On the other hand, only a very few of them are even aware of such things as "Ether Ships" or the etheric realms.

So the Discs will have to do their own talking. This they are doing more and more. Some of the true story will be told to the "mass-minded" in the late Spring of 1956. Our Space Friends—for such in truth they are—will then gently help our fellow humans on Earth to "grow up" in short order, by presenting thousands of Earthlings with objective "phenomena" that simply can't be explained away. Time, as you know, is short. We are living in the prophesied"time of the End". It is time for a CHANGE.

Fortunately, our planetary Guardians are waking us up. They are filling our skies with an ever increasing number of space ships from many different Densities. "Contacts" by Earthlings like George Adamski, Truman Bethurum, Orfeo Angelucci, Dan Frey, and others, with the Space People are becoming commonplace. We are learning to face " "reality" and the tempo of this learning is being stepped-up dramatically by our great teachers.

In the coming years, people on Earth will tremble with fear of "the things that are coming upon the Earth". . . . You, however, will not tremble. In those moments of terrible darkness and indecision, you will not panic. We who believe in God understand that he created ALL the heavens and the Earth. By "heavens" we understand that to mean the entire universe all the way out to the last star. This includes planets beyond planets, suns beyond suns, solar systems beyond solar systems, galaxies beyond galaxies.

Too, we know that means the UNSEEN WORLDS as well as the seen. Let us accept the Creator in His fullness...in all His Infinite Glory. When we do this, and we shall--what would we have to fear? In truth, there is nothing at all to fear. The entire universe is FOR man, not against him. All things work together for GOOD, and even though the Earth itself be "removed out of her place" so that she "reels to and fro like a drunkard"...still our hearts shall NOT fail us. Intelligence, not chaos, rules the universe.

And it is the intelligence in you that can and will protect you now and in the perilous days to come, just as it has always stood by to direct you during serious times in the past. You have done nobly well, and my only suggestion would be to practice living more and more from your own Soul-Center of _Life, Love_ and _Light_ in your daily activities. Therein lies your only true security.

Of course, many of the Space People are your friends. This includes many of the Ethereans as well. They are spiritually evolved enough to know that all evil is self-destructive and consequently of no use whatsoever to the illumined soul. However, evil is by no means confined to planet Earth exclusively. Wherever life exists, there also exists the possibility of misusing that life. Hence we can expect to find evil-doers on any planet, no matter how highly advanced or evolved the people of that planet might be. While it is true the majority of the Visitors from Space are constructively minded, there are a few who are not. And it is for this reason that we must "test" every being whom we contact (or who contacts us) to find out if he is on the side of Cosmic Good or mere personal gain.

I believe that in this Monograph I have givin you a new and more comprehensive picture of THE REAL YOU and your ever-unfolding spiritual destiny. We have delved deeply into the ancient lore of that mystic Land known as ETHERIA. We've seen how the Ethereans are able to function efficiently in their Etheric Realms, by living there according to the physical, mental and spiritual laws of their higher dimensional worlds. We have uncovered much of the mystery surrounding ETHER SHIPS, learned why they are necessary, and we have caught a glimpse of our own great and wondrous journey to the stars.

We've come to know that your journey and mine, is ever Onward, Upward and Godward...from Density to Density...higher and higher... until at last one day our minds comprehend Creation in its grandly magnificent aspects. Then we will have returned on the "ingoing wave" to the One Still Light at the center of All.

oooOOOooo

Discs, Destiny & You

by

MICHAEL X

Mystic Monograph No.5

A   P E R S O N A L   N O T E

Dear Friend and Mystic Student:

In this Monograph, "DISCS, DESTINY & YOU", we study a subject of vital interest and importance to all of us. That is, the COMING COLLOSAL CHANGES which our planet Terra (and its 3 billion people) are due to experience between now and the Golden Millenium we are joyously awaiting.

Your Destiny during the next 44 years will be far more thrilling, enlightening, and "adventurous" than you--at this moment--can possibly imagine. Yes. It will be a wonderful Destiny, because of the profound influence for good the Space People are going to have on your life from now on.....in spite of the "changes" that must transpire.

The secret of staying "alive" (that is, in physical embodiment) from now on, even through the eventual crisis to come, is to change your thought and keep it changed. For those who start at once improving their mental world by thinking along the lines of Love, Life, Truth and Beauty, the future will be exceedingly bright. Few of the unpleasant things, such as the cataclysmic changes impending, or the axial SHIFT of the earth as revealed in these pages, will even affect those whose feet are on the glorious Mystic Path leading Upward.

Positive Thought-Control, however, is imperative. The old mental patterns of fear, negation, and destructive emotion, cannot be taken into the coming Millenium, which will be the INTERPLANETARY AGE. As space flight becomes a reality to Earthlings, a New Order of thinking will awaken on Earth, in which we will have related ourselves more perfectly to the magnificent purposes of the Creator of all Life.

Yours in Truth and Love,

Michael X

MICHAEL X

Flying Saucer Revelations

"DISCS, DESTINY AND YOU"

Part One

The Polar Shift

Flying Discs, the Space People, and our Earth's polar "shift", are all related in a most interesting way, to your Destiny. Destiny is that which is irrevocable. That is, it is an experience or combination of experiences which you must become "aware" of as you move forward in consciousness.

Death, for example, is a form of destiny which all mankind (with the exception of a very few Adepts) learns to accept mentally. In fact, race thought has it that death is inevitable for all living creatures. Those who study the mystic science of mind, life, and spirit, learn that destiny is not always "unchangeable". We can be "Masters of Fate".

Occult science defines destiny as "necessity"; that which must be or happen as the result of what has been thought and said or done in the past or present time. Your destiny, then, has little or nothing to do with "stars" or where you happen to live, or even whom you happen to meet "by chance". Instead, we create our own individual destinies day by day, moment by moment--BY THE KIND OF THOUGHTS WE THINK.

Change your mind--your "consciousness"--and you change your destiny. The idea is to change your thoughts from negative to positive, from destructive to constructive, and by so doing you are creating a NEW "chain of events" that will brighten your tomorrows. We can never hope to enjoy happy experiences in the future unless we lay the foundations today, by our present thoughts and actions.

Many students of the Inner Teachings believe in an "ultimate destiny". That is, they feel that some day, some time, they will experience a FINAL or LAST destiny. For some persons the ultimate destiny would be to attain "Cosmic Consciousness" or to be absorbed in an ecstatic, blissful state of "Nirvana". According to the Space People, man has NO ultimate or final destiny. There is no such thing as FINALITY in all the Cosmos. We do, however, have an INFINITE DESTINY. You and I are now thinking beings. As a result of our thoughts, we are continually creating a moving "Succession" of destinies for ourselves. Since you never cease "unfolding", how could there be a final destiny?

Once you realize this, you instantly become more of a master over yourself and over life itself. The principle of it all is utterly simple and sensible. One doesn't have to go anywhere else or seek somebody outside of himself, to bring about this INNER Change of Consciousness. One has merely to ask himself (or herself) "Which

Flying Saucer Revelations

do I serve? Good or Evil? The Unlimited or the Limited?" In your choice lies your Destiny-to-be.

Good is unlimited in its scope of action, whereas Evil tends to destroy itself. One is an expanding force; the other contracting. If you contract anything, it soon dies. Life simply refuses to be confined, restricted or contracted in any way. The tendency of the entire Universe is E-X-P-A-N-S-I-O-N. We live in an "expanding universe". In this principle is found the real key to abundant living.

I mention these things because they do have an important bearing on your own Destiny, which will soon be apparent to you. At this particular moment, time is "of the essence". In order to properly construct the best kind of destiny for yourself in this changing world, it is necessary to know the facts.

Occultists have long known of the existence of "planetary cycles". Ancient Hindu writings such as the Book of Dzyan, describe these cycles in detail. It seems that each planet, including our Earth, experiences a number of "axial shifts" during its lifetime. These shifts occur with a certain regularity, which the ancients claim to have measured with some degree of exactness. For example, "Racial Cycles" which measure the progress of man on Earth, are figured in a Minor Cycle (2500--3000 years) and a Major Cycle (26,000 years). Racial Cycles are related to Planetary Cycles.

A Planetary Cycle covers a period of 7200 years (round numbers). It is at the end of this period that the axis of the Earth makes a sudden SHIFT, causing the land to slide under the oceans at terrific speed, and tearing away mountains and covering forests. This happened not once, but many times ages ago, which fact accounts for our present coal beds. Also, it accounts for the presence of Mammoths (a tropical animal) being frozen in mountains of ice in the far north regions. The Mammoth belongs to the Elephant family, and elephants have an intense dislike for cold weather. Their natural habitat is in tropical regions, such as Africa and India. What history books call the "Glacial Period" or the "Ice Age", was a planetary condition which resulted from a polar shift.

This idea of a periodic "Polar Shift" was first brought to my attention by George Van Tassel during my last visit with him at Giant Rock. I think it would not be amiss to briefly review what was mentioned then. It was George's understanding that our Earth is now approaching the mid-point between a Minor and a Major Cycle. This seems to indicate that our planet is nearing the end of a Planetary Cycle (7200 years). The time remaining until the end of this Cycle is reached, is not exactly known; however, there is some evidence to the effect that this cycle will terminate within 45 years from today.

This does not mean that our world will "come to an end" at that time. Not at all. A periodic shift of the Earth's axis should occur at that time, just as it happened in the long-since-forgotten past.

Quite true, for a great number of people it will be the "end of the world", for they will not survive the tremendous planetary cataclysm.

The Space People, George said, are well aware of the Polar Shift that is in the offing. They realize fully that the general effect of atomic explosions on Earth is to hasten the "Time of the End", for the simple reason that--as Sir Isaac Newton observed--"For every action there is an opposite and equal reaction". Shoot a gun and the gun "kicks" back. Explode a Hydrogen Bomb on the Earth's surface and the Earth must also "react" by oscillating or "wobbling" more in its orbit. This has already occurred.

The "wobble" takes place at the extreme ends of the earth where the polar ice caps are located. This ice forms a mountain two miles high. In fact, both the North and the South Poles are surrounded by many millions of square miles of polar ice. As the earth spins around describing its large orbit, the polar ice caps also rotate..but in small eccentric ellipse. This small "eccentric orbit" is spread out over the larger one. Therefore the Earth actually describes TWO orbits AT THE SAME TIME, in place of merely one. Now, if we increase the diameter of the smaller orbit, what happens?

The "gyroscopic" action of the earth increases, does it not? As a result, the polar ice caps MELT AT A MUCH FASTER RATE. When those "mountains of ice" two miles high, begin to melt rapidly they SHIFT THEIR WEIGHT. This condition causes definite land and climatical changes to occur all over the Earth.

The severe polar shift occurs when the "wobble" of the poles reaches an extreme or maximum state of imbalance. Then, like a gyroscope trying to right itself, a sudden BIG SHIFT takes place and land crumples and slides under the oceans with violent speed.

George Van Tassel believes that this is the time referred to in the Christian Bible as "The Father's house-cleaning among the planets". During this critical time of the "Great Shift", or immediately before this world event, our friends from space will descend in their Flying Discs and other Space Ships, to rescue all deserving humanity.

There is a story told of Abe Lincoln that seems to be appropriate at this point. As you know, the woods are full of "false prophets" who go about predicting the "end of the world". Usually, when the prophesied time arrives, nothing happens...and the Earth keeps on rolling around just as if it hadn't any idea that--according to prophecy--it was supposed to "be consumed" in one way or another.

One day a group of Lincoln's friends ran up to him in great excitement, exclaiming, "The world is coming to an end! The world is coming to an end!"

Honest Abe didn't appear the least bit disturbed by the news. His friends tried again to impress the situation on his mind.

"Don't you understand?" they shouted, "The whole world is coming to an end NOW!"

Lincoln looked them in the eye. "That's all right, boys," he said. "I can get along without the world!"

We can learn much from Lincoln's calm reaction to "startling" news. It tells us that he had found his own spiritual center of serenity which nothing outside of himself could shake...for his REAL SELF was IMMORTAL.

****

A VISION OF THE IMPENDING

"Destruction is but the prelude to Renewal:
Death is but the portal to Life;
Even truth also must be made new,
Behold, I saw the Heaven in a blaze of purity,
And I saw the EARTH absorbed into an Abyss.
THE ROLLING SPHERE INCLINED!

"The moment of destruction was at hand.
Mountains suspended over mountains;
Hills sinking upon hills;
Lofty trees toppled headlong;
They sank downwards into chasms."

--The Book of Enoch

SPECIAL NOTE

Due to the unusual and Occult nature of the various subjects presented in MYSTIC Monographs, they should be considered as confidential. The purchaser is requested to maintain the ancient Occult Law of Silence as regards all Secret Knowledge, lest it fall into unworthy hands. If you do wish to lend them to close friends, first ascertain the sincerity of the one desiring this knowledge.   The Author.

"DISCS, DESTINY & YOU"

Part Two

Your Secret Destiny

As soon as I became aware that a "shift" in the axis of the earth was impending, I at once began a diligent search for more facts. What I found was, to say the least, as astounding as it was enlightening. All of the ancient esoteric teachings were in agreement on one momentous and important thing:

THE AXIS OF THIS EARTH PERIODICALLY INCLINES AT A 45 DEGREE ANGLE TO THE PLANE OF ITS ORBIT, AND IT HAS GONE THROUGH FOUR SUCH INCLINATIONS DURING PAST AGES.

Or, to put it more simply, the axis of rotation shifts suddenly, causing the earth to tip at an angle of 45 degrees. Ever since the first dawn of creation, man has observed that our globe has a unique "cyclical" life of its own. That is why the belief is expressed in nearly all the old writings (history, mythology, philosophy and Occult manuscripts) that this Earth has passed through a series of time cycles, each cycle ending in a "planetary convulsion" such as a violent earthquake, a flood, volcanic fire explosion, etc. The Deluge is but one instance.

The Rosicrucians firmly believe that the earth inclines or "tips" at regular intervals. They have given us much valuable literature on this vital subject, and I heartily recommend that you look into the late Max Heindel's book, "The Rosicrucian Cosmo-Conception" for much worthwhile information on this. A copy of the book can usually be obtained at your public library, or from an Occult book store.

As we have noted previously in another Monograph of this series, fire and water alternately destroy the continents of Earth. The active agents in this destruction being earthquakes, volcanoes, tornadoes, sinkings and displacements of the various land areas. These periodical cataclysms of our planet do not, however, happen without warning. In every case of the earth "shifting" on its axis and tipping sharply, humanity is kindly given a number of "warnings" beforehand. I refer, of course, to incessant earthquakes and volcanic eruptions which occur years in advance of the major devastating "shift."

Commentaries in the Secret Doctrine mention one of these events as follows:

"The great mother (Earth) travailed under the waves and a new land was joined to the first one which our wise men called the head-gear (North Pole). She travailed harder for the third (race) and her waist and navel appeared above the water. It was the belt, the sacred Himavat, which stretches around the world. She broke toward the setting sun from her neck downward (to the southwest) into many lands and islands, but the eternal land (the cap) broke not asunder. Dry lands covered the face of the silent waters to the four sides of the world. All these perished. Then appeared the abode of the wicked (Atlantis). The eternal land was now hid, for the waters became solid (frozen) under the breath of her nostrils and evil winds from the Dragon's mouth," etc., etc.

This account as well as all of the other old and dusty manuscripts which describe the periodical tip of the earth, reveal the ancient belief that the North Pole was our first and original continent on Earth. At the beginning of creation, the "eternal land" was NOT a place of ice and snow as it is today. Instead, it was a veritable tropical paradise, much like the State of Florida is now.

The original "Garden of Eden"--where man was first created on this planet--was located in that continent at the North Pole. Later came the great "polar shift", reversing the climatic conditions completely, and freezing the tropical Mammoth Elephant in mountains of ice two miles high.

Delving still deeper into the ancient books, we find another astounding manuscript on this intensely fascinating subject. It is the Commentary of an old Buddhist Faith as cited by Blavatsky:

"When the wheel (Earth) runs at the usual rate, its extremities (the poles) agree with its middle circle (equator). When it runs slower and tilts in every direction, there is a great disturbance on the face of the earth. The waters flow toward the two ends, and new lands arise in the middle belt, while those at the ends are subject to pralayas (cleansing) by submersion."

You have quite likely heard of the "Book of Enoch". It is a Biblical book, yet it pre-dates our Bible by millions of years. Some Bible commentators refer to it as the "Book of Adam", for they are of the opinion that Adam wrote it. One chapter is titled "A Sermon to the Sons of Men". It seems to be describing a vision of THE COMING CRISIS of our planet, now impending. I quote:

"Yet all this starry firmament of beauty shall pass away, and cease to be in the days to come; they shall be changed by FIRE; they shall be renovated by WATER, as of old in the olden time. GOD shall come forth out of the places afar off; He will tread upon the mountains, and the mountains shall give way under Him, and the valleys shall be made straight before His feet, and the pillars of the earth shall be shaken; the Voice of the Supreme shall be heard; the mighty Heaven shall hear and tremble; the sea and waves shall quake with terror.

"The sun shall not be visible; the moon shall also withold her light; but there shall be NO DEATH, NOR ANY DESTRUCTION: but all shall be renovated and made more beautiful than ever."--Book of Enoch.

It is difficult to see how there would be no death for the masses of humankind when the earth next tips at a 45 degree angle. I think we may safely interpret that passage to mean there shall be no death

Flying Saucer Revelations

FOR THE ELECT of "Enlightened" and spiritual people...who are now
launched on the UPWARD PATH.

That, in fact, is your SECRET DESTINY. You and I and an ever-
increasing number of sincere individuals--men, women and children in
all walks of life--can be comforted in the knowledge that, when the
time of the "Great Tribulation" comes (and no man knoweth the day
nor the hour) many wise and highly spiritual beings will descend to
this planet in Flying Discs. Their purpose: to preserve as many
human beings in the physical state as possible. All else will find
no protection.

The Space People from Venus (the planet which represents our
Earth's "higher self") are God's messengers of Light. We should
trust them, as we would trust God. That is to say, we should embrace
the help they offer whenever they choose to offer it. And we need
NOT fear them, nor need we live in dread of the next polar shift,
for:

"God is our refuge and strength, a very present help in trouble.
Therefore will we NOT FEAR, though the Earth be removed, and though
the mountains be carried into the midst of the sea; though the waters
thereof roar and be troubled, though the mountains shake with the
SWELLING thereof.". . . . . .Psalm 46: 1-3

That advice is from our own Bible, and I am sure you recognize
it. Also, I do trust that its real meaning is conveyed to you more
clearly than when you previously read it. The connection between the
Space People, that is, the Venusians, and the "Polar Shift" is seen
in another Biblical passage:

"And when these things begin to come to pass, then LOOK UP, and
LIFT UP YOUR HEADS; for your redemption (protection) draweth nigh."
                                            Luke 21: 28

What does this mean? It means that our "way of escape" from
destruction in the Dark Night of Tribulation, is simply not to stay
on the earth during the cataclysm, but to allow our friends (the
Space People) to lift us up off the planet in their Space Ships.

When the earth has once again righted itself, and the sun and
moon again show their light...we shall be returned safely to this
planet, to experience the glorious Millenium. In the words of our
own Bible, "Then we which are alive and remain (in the flesh) shall
be caught up together with them in the clouds, to meet the Lord in
the air; and so shall we ever be with the Lord." (That is, under the
guiding influence of the Venusians). . . . . . .Thess. 4: 16, 17

Those of us who are fully aware of the possibility of this
event coming to pass in the not too distant future, will not hesitate
to prepare ourselves mentally, physically and spiritually for it...
NOW.

Flying Saucer Revelations

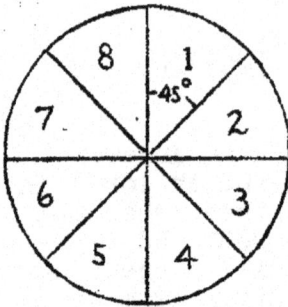

Bozena Brydlova, author of a most enlightening book entitled, "The Brydlovan Theory of the Origin of Numbers", gives us much valuable information on the Great Shift:

"All the data contained within the old philosophies teach us that man attained his development in Cycles, beginning with senseless innocence and purity, and gradually developing from acquired materialism AFTER EACH TIP OF THE EARTH, into a state of degradation. When the lowest state of degradation has been reached, the wheel starts its way UPWARD and once more humanity treads the UPWARD PATH, higher with each tip of the axis, until the time that ALL are gathered to the One Cause thru their spiritual attainment of purity. Precise figures as to the length of time from tip to tip give us 7200 years. Dividing the cosmic circle into 45 degree angles, we find four on one side and four on the other. True it is that mankind could hardly reach a lower state of humanity than the world has witnessed in the past thousand years, but as we are said to be now in the FIFTH "sun" (fifth age), we can be comforted by the knowledge that we are NOW launched on the UPWARD PATH."

If this theory is correct, our earth has four more "tips" to make before it finally "etherializes", that is, turns into a sun.

What we call the "Millenium" was called the "Sibylline year" by Virgil. In his 4th Eclogue, he refers to the next tip of the earth.. and to the Millenium to follow:

"The last period sung by the Sibylline prophetess is now arrived and the grand series of Ages, that series which recurs again and again in the course of one mundane revolution, begins afresh. Now the Virgin Astraea returns from Heaven, and the primaeval reign of Venus recommences. Now a new race descends (in space ships) from the celestial realms of holiness. Do thou, Lucina, smile propituous on the birth of a Boy who will bring to a close the present age of Iron, and introduce throughout the whole world a new Age of Gold. Then shall the herds no longer dread the fury of the lion, nor shall the poison of the serpent any longer be formidable.

"Every venomous animal and every deleterious plant shall perish together. (As a result of the next axial shift). The fields shall be yellow with corn; the grapes shall hand in ruddy clusters from the bramble, and honey shall distill spontaneously from the rugged oak. The universal globe shall enjoy the blessings of PEACE, secure under the mild sway of its new and divine sovereign."

Delving back still further into the manuscripts of the ancients, we come to the Koran of the Mohammedans. Here again we find a descriptive account of the next "shift": "The earth shall be SHAKEN, and not only all the buildings, but THE VERY MOUNTAINS LEVELED, and THE HEAVENS MELTED, etc."

Flying Saucer Revelations

To banish whatever trace of skepticism yet remains in your mind, as to the actual TRUTH of the several "axial shifts" already made by our planet, consider the following:

On the great Sahara desert, sea-shells in numerous quantities can be found today...showing that this vast desert was formerly the bottom of an ancient ocean.

Yet another instance of this is found in Wyoming. Certain portions of that state are filled with petrified sea-shells; again proving that this now arid land was once an ocean bed. So we see that the "Great Shift" of the earth upon its axis, really did happen in the dim, bygone past...and not just once, but many times. At least four to date.

But what about NOW...today? Exactly what is happening to this planet right now? Fate Magazine for April 1955, on page 8, gave us some amazing data, which I quote:

"A slip amounting to about 75 feet a year has been detected between the earth's outer skin and her inner core. Whatthis may mean isn't known exactly, but it could help explain the suggested SHIFTING OF THE CONTINENTS under the continental drift theory.

"And besides all this, THE EARTH IS SHOWING AN INCREASING TIP IN HER AXIS. At present the pole seems to be shifting only about a centimeter a year...nearly 100 years to shift a yard...but the TILT SEEMS TO BE INCREASING and some estimates place the change as much as 10 centimeters a year.

"All this has been reported by Dr. Roger R. Revelle of the U.S. National Research Council and Dr. Walter H. Munk of the Scripps Institute of Oceanography, both of La Jolla, California."

This condition of the planet is causing drastic weather changes all over the globe. In 1953, William J. Baxter made a study of these climatic changes, and published his findings in a book titled, "Today's Revolution in The Weather". So popular was the book it sold 225,000 copies. In that book, Mr. Baxter brought the world weather situation to the attention of human beings everywhere. Now he has written an entirely new book on the same theme, entitled, "Warmer Weather!...Boom in North!" His thought is as follows:

"IT ISN'T 'JUST YOUR IMAGINATION'! Winters are getting warmer; summers are hotter, drier, more unbearable. Every scientific study, every anxious report from worried farmers, bankers, ranchers, fruit growers, retailers, real estate and utility men confirms it. The CLIMATE OF THE WHOLE NORTHERN HEMISPHERE IS CHANGING DRASTICALLY. And here in the United States and Canada, we are on the verge of the greatest revolution in agriculture, industry and daily living that has ever been known."

We, as students of life's deeper secrets, can look back of these "outer effects" and see the occult (that is, hidden) reasons for all the changes. We realize that a NEW NORTH POLE is coming about. (This fact throws ocean navigators many miles off course when charting by means of the old maps, which are now virtually obsolete).

Yes, Earth is wobbling on her axis. A new "Polar Shift" is due. The precise date of the shift remains of course, a cosmic secret. But we know the great event is not too far in the distant future. What is happening in and on the earth at this very moment logically foretells the mighty upheavals of Nature that will take place when the sudden shift comes. A probable date is any time between now and the year 2000 A.D., when the Golden Age of the Millenium begins.

We know the coming shift is scientifically predictable, just as it is now scientifically possible to predict solar eclipses, weather conditions, high and low tides, the next date when a certain comet will appear in our skies, etc. etc., so is it possible to calculate with a high degree of accuracy when the next SHIFT of our planet will occur. In our opinion the greatest authority on this vital subject is Mr. Adam D. Barber of Washington D.C. Mr. Barber is an attorney at law, who has experimented with and studied the gyroscopic action of our solar system for over twenty years. This led him to the discovery of our earth's periodic shift, coming soon, which will bring upon humanity a catastrophe of major proportions. If you have not yet read his book, "THE COMING DISASTER", I strongly urge you to send for a copy of it now. The price is only $1.00. The information it contains will prove of superlative value to you in the days ahead. To get your copy of Mr. Barber's book, send one dollar to the following address: BARBER SCIENTIFIC FOUNDATION. P.O. BOX 3254, Washington 10, D.C.

If you are diligent in your application of New Age truths from now on, you will quite likely reach the Millenium "in the flesh", and get safely past the "shift" without the slightest bit of physical harm coming to you during the whole thrilling experience. But you must see to it that the "coverings of the Light" are removed from your mind and spirit. Then you shall know yourself as a true Godlike being and be ready to take your place in the Age of Peace, Power and Plenty.

In the days to come, you will be guided in THE WAY you are to go for your safety and further progress. Much hidden knowledge and valuable instruction will be given you...often in quite strange and, yes, mysterious ways; but always at THE time when you need guidance most. Hence, you need not concern yourself unduly with the future. The Space Masters have told us that our lives must function from the SOUL CENTER within us...NOW, in this eternal instant of Time...which has no beginning and no end. We are Eternal Beings, sublimely "centered" in the One All-Seeing Mind within. Outer events cannot shake us nor destroy what is forever unshakable and indestructible.

I say to you sincerely, you have unlimited majesty within you. Release it. For your future is as BIG as the Universe is boundless, and as grand as the dreams and hungering demand of your waking Soul.

oooOOOooo

Flying Saucer Revelations

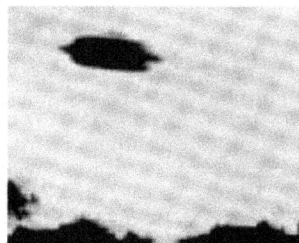

- 146 -

Flying Saucer Revelations

Flying Saucer Revelations

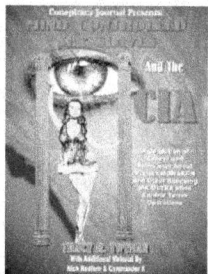

www.ingramcontent.com/pod-product-compliance
Lightning Source LLC
Chambersburg PA
CBHW062101090426
42741CB00015B/3302